S(

*2 Books in 1: Beginner's Guide & ,
Day Crash Course, How to Quickly
Learn Structured Query Language
Programming, Server Administration,
Computer and Database Management
Step-by-Step*

hardships that may result from any of the information discussed herein.

Additionally, the information in the following pages is intended only for informational purposes and should thus be thought of as universal. As befitting its nature, it is presented without assurance regarding its prolonged validity or interim quality. Trademarks that are mentioned are done without written consent and can in no way be considered an endorsement from the trademark holder.

Table of Contents

Book 1

Book 2

7

SQL Programming

The Ultimate Beginner's Guide to Structured Query Language Coding for Databases, Including MySQL, Microsoft SQL Server, Oracle and Access

Preface

What is SQL?

The SQL (the Structured Query Language, Structured Query Language) is a special language used to define data, provide access to data and their processing. **The SQL language** refers to nonprocedural languages - it only describes the necessary components (for example, tables) and the desired results, without specifying how these results should be obtained. Each **SQL** implementation is an add-on on the database engine, which interprets **SQL statements** and determines the order of accessing the database structures for the correct and effective formation of the desired result.

SQL to Work with Databases?

To process the request, the database server translates **SQL** commands into internal procedures. Due to the fact that **SQL** hides the details of data processing, it is easy to use.

You can use SQL to help out in the following ways:

- **SQL** helps when you want to create tables based on the data you have.
- **SQL** can store the data that you collect.
- **SQL** can look at your database and retrieves the information on there.

- **SQL** allows you to modify data.
- **SQL** can take some of the structures in your database and change them up.
- **SQL** allows you to combine data.
- **SQL** allows you to perform calculations.
- **SQL** allows data protection.

Client and Server Technology

When using client-server technology, the application is divided into two parts. The client part provides a convenient graphical interface and is located on the user's computer. The server part provides data management, information sharing, administration and ensures the security of information. The client application generates requests to the database server on which the corresponding commands are executed. Query results are sent to the client.

When developing distributed information systems in the organization of interaction between the client and server parts, the following important tasks in a practical sense are distinguished:

- Transfer of a personal database to a server for its subsequent collective use as a corporate database;
- Organization of requests from one end of the client over to the company's database will help make sure that the client will receive the right results.
- Development of a client application for remote access to a corporate database from a client computer.

The task of transferring a personal database to a server may arise in situations when it is necessary to provide collective access to a database developed using a personal DBMS (FoxPro, Access). To solve this problem, these personal DBMSs have the appropriate tools designed to convert databases to SQL format.

The preparation of queries to the database on the server (in SQL) from the client-side can be performed using a specially designed utility. To provide the user with great opportunities and convenience in preparing and executing requests, client applications are created.

To organize queries to a server database in SQL or using a client application, various methods of interaction are possible that significantly affect efficiency. The main ways of such interaction include:

- Interface DB-LIB (database libraries);
- ODBC technologies (open database compatibility);
- OLE DB interface (linking and embedding database objects);
- DAO technologies (data access objects);
- ADO technologies (data objects).

The DB-LIB interface is an application programming interface specifically designed for SQL. Therefore, it is the least mobile among those considered in the sense of the possibility of transferring applications to another environment. In terms of performance, this method allows the fastest access to information. The reason for this is that it represents an optimized application programming interface and directly uses the SQL system query language.

ODBC technologies are designed to provide the possibility of interconnection between different DBMSs and to receive requests from the application to retrieve information, translate them into the core language of the addressable database to access the information stored in it.

The main purpose of ODBC is to abstract the application from the features of the core of the server database with which it interacts, so the server database becomes as if transparent to any client application.

The advantage of this technology is the simplicity of application development, due to the high level of abstractness of the data access interface of almost any existing DBMS types. Using this technology, it is possible to create client-server applications, and it is advisable to develop the client part of the application using personal DBMS tools and the server part using SQL tools.

The main disadvantage of ODBC technology is the need to translate queries, which reduces the speed of data access. On client-server systems, this drawback is eliminated by moving the request from the client computer to the server computer. This eliminates the intermediate links, which are the main reason for reducing the speed of information processing using the tools of this technology.

When using ODBC tools in a client application, a specific data source is accessed, and through it, to the DBMS that it represents. When installing ODBC tools, the common ODBC subsystem is installed and the "driver-database" pairs are defined, which are the names used to establish the connection with. database. Corresponding pairs are called named data sources.

Each named data source describes the actual data source and information about access to this data. The data can be databases, spreadsheets and text files. Access information, for example, to a database server, usually includes server location information, database name, account ID and password, as well as various driver parameters that describe how you should establish the right kinds of connections to your source of data.

When processing data on a server using ODBC technology and using a client application, two main stages are distinguished: setting a data source - creating and configuring a connection, as well as actually processing data using queries.

It is usually best if you are able to work with the OLE DB interface to create tools and utilities, or system-level developments that require high performance or access to SQL properties that are not available using ADO technology. Key features of the OLE DB specification provide full data access functionality. In SQL, the server database processor uses this interface for communication: between internal components, such as the storage processor and the relationship processor; Between SQL installations using remote stored procedures as an interface to other data sources for distributed queries.

When using OJSC technology, work with databases and tables is carried out using collections of objects. This provides great convenience in working with database objects.

At present, the technology of JSC is gradually superseded by ADO technology, which allows you to develop Web applications for working with databases. In general, ADO technology can be described as the most advanced application development technology for working with distributed client-server technology databases.

Chapter 1: A Look At The Basics of SQL

Many companies have to spend some time finding ways to store all of the data that they want to work with. This data is such an important part of how they will run their business and the amount of success that they are going to find, that they know it is one of the best ways to help them get ahead.

Thanks to the modern world of technology we are currently in, there are a ton of resources out there to provide us with some of the data that we are looking for. This data can be used by companies in so many ways. It can help them to learn how to reach their customers better, how to make better decisions, how to reduce some of the waste that they see on a regular basis in their business, and how to beat out the competition.

Gathering up the data that is needed is not going to be the hardest part. In fact, often the hardest part of all of this is figuring out the best way to store it, and then figuring out how you are able to take that information and actually sort through it, and make it work for your needs. One of the methods that can help with this is a database.

These databases are able to hold onto large amounts of information and can sort through it as well. But when you have millions of potential points of data that you want to sort, compare, and more, it is going to seem like a huge undertaking. And this is where the SQL language is going to come into play as well. Let's dive into what this language is all about, and why it is so important to helping us to achieve our goals with all of that data.

A Look at SQL

The first thing that you need to ask is what is SQL. SQL is going to stand for Structured Query Language and it is a pretty basic language that you can use in order to interact with the different databases that are on your system. The original version did come out in the 70s, but it had really started to see some changes when IBM released a new prototype that released SQL to the world.

This first particular tool was called ORACLE and it was so successful that the part of the company that worked with ORACLE was able to break off from IBM and started off on their own. ORACLE is still one of the leaders in the programming language field because it works with SQL and continuously makes it easier for people to learn how to work with the database.

Working with the Database

When we decide to spend some of our time looking at these databases and working with some of the neat things that are available with the SQL language, you will find that the database is simple, and will just hold onto groups of information. Sometimes we are going to think of these as mechanisms that will only hold onto the information that the user is able to access when they would like but other times it is going to come into play and will help a business to get ahold of the information that they need, without having to worry about some other potential issues showing up as well.

There are going to be times when you would want to bring out the database, and working with SQL, even if you didn't realize it at the time, can help you to work through this process. For example, if you have gone through and looked for a product on one of your favorite websites, then you are used to some of the ideas that come with this SQL and all that it is able to do to make things easier for you. It will help to sort through the perhaps millions of items on that website and will make it easier for you to really see some of the results that you would like.

With this in mind, we do need to take a look at some of the other information that we can use, and the different parts that are going to come with the databases that we are able to use when it comes to the SQL language.

Relational Database

The first type of database that we are going to talk about is a relational database. These are ones that are going to be segregated into tables or logical units. These tables can be interconnected inside of the database so that they make sense based on what you are working on at the time. The database is going to also make it easier to break up the data into some smaller units so that you are able to manage them easier and they will be optimized for making things easier on you.

It is important to know about the relational database because it is going to help to keep all your information together, but it does help to split it up so that the pieces are small enough to read through easier. The server will be able to go through all of these parts to see what you need because the smaller pieces are easier to go through compared to the bigger pieces. Because of the optimization and the efficiency that is found in this kind of system, it is common to see a lot of businesses going with this option instead of another one.

Client and Server Technology

For quite a while, a lot of the computers that were being used in the business industry were considered mainframe computers. This means that the machines were holding a large system that was great for processing as well as storing information. The user was able to use these computers in order to interact with the mainframe using what was done with a dumber terminal, or one that doesn't think on their own. In order to get all the right functions to perform, the dumb terminals are going to rely on the memory, storage, and processor that are inside of the computer.

While these systems worked and there isn't anything wrong with this setup (many companies even still use them to help get things done in their business), there is a better solution that will get the job done faster and more efficiently than you will find with the mainframe option.

The client/server systems will use a slightly different process in order to get the results that you would like. The main computer, also known as the server, can be accessed by the user that is on the network; for the most part, they are going to have a WAN or a LAN network that will help them to access the network. The user will be able to access this server with a desktop computer, as well as another server, rather than having to use the old dumb terminals. Every computer, which will be known as the client inside of this system, will be able to access this system, which can make it easier to have interaction between any clients and the server to get things done.

Internet-Based Database Systems

While the client to server kind of technology is widely popular and has worked well for a lot of people to use over time, you will also find that there are some programmers who have decided to add in some databases that are going to have more integration with the internet. This kind of system is going to allow the user to access the database when they go online, so they will be able to use their own personal web browser in order to check this out when they would like.

Along with this, the customer can go and check out the data if they would like, and they can even go online and make some changes to the account, check on the transactions that are there, check out the inventories, and purchase items. They can even make payments online if this is all set up in the right manner. thanks to acting that we are able to base some of our databases online, we will find that it is possible to go online and let the customer access this database, even from their own home.

To help us work with these databases, we will just need to pick out the kind of web browser that we would like to go with, and then head on over to the website of the company that we go with. At times, you may need to have some credentials to get onto the account, but that is going to depend on the requirements of the company at the time. Then you can work with the search function in order to find some of the information hats you would like on the database.

You may find that a lot of these online databases are going to require us to have a login to have any kind of access, especially if there is some kind of payment requirement that goes with them. This may seem like a pain to work with, but it does add in some of that extra security that you are looking for to make sure your personal and financial information is always safe.

Of course, we have to remember that while this may seem like a simple and easy to handle kind of database, there are actually quite a few things that are showing up behind the scenes in order to make sure that the database is going to work. We have to make sure the database is working properly and that the right commands are being sent out at the right times to ensure we can reach our accounts, find the products we want, look at our order history, and more.

For example, we may see that the web browser that we want to work with at any given time is able to use and also execute the SQL in order to make sure that it is showing any of the data and information that the user would like to see. SQL is going to be used to help reach the database that the customer is looking for, such as clothing or food that they are interested in seeing, and then SQL is going to send this information right back to the website before showing it to the user in that browser.

This sounds pretty complicated in the beginning, but you will find that it is actually going to be really easy to work with and can get done in just a few minutes if the program is set up in the proper manner. all of the things that we have been able to discuss with SQL so far will ensure that we are able to make a simple search or something else similar happen in no time at all. SQL can really make it that simple.

The Benefits of Using SQL

And finally, we need to spend some time taking a look at some of the advantages that we are going to see when it comes to using the SQL language to help us sort through all of the information that may be found in our database. There are actually a few other options that we can use when we would like to sort through a database that we want to work with. But SQL is going to often be the one that is chosen because it is easy to use, works well with databases in particular, and so much more.

There are a ton of benefits that you will be able to enjoy when it comes to working with SQL for some of your database programming needs. And using this is going to ensure that you are able to make sure that your database is set up and ready to go. Some of the many benefits that you will be able to notice when it comes to working with this kind of language will include:

- **High speed**—if you are looking for something that is a high speed, the SQL option is one of the best. The SQL queries are able to retrieve a lot of information from the database in just a little bit of time and it is one of the most efficient options that you are able to use on the market to get this done.

- **Well defined standards**—the SQL databases have been around for some time and they have some good standards that will help to make it easier to keep the database nice and strong. Some of the other databases don't have these clear standards and it can make it difficult to store the information that you need.

- **No coding needed**—you are able to use the SQL system in order to store some of the information for your business without knowing a lot of coding ahead of time. You will learn a few parts of coding inside of this guidebook to do the right commands, but you don't need to have extensive knowledge of coding before getting started.

- **The emergence of object**-oriented DBMS—the earlier SQL databases were based on the relational databases and while this is not a bad thing, there are some better and faster options. Now they are moving on to some of the newer options to help get the work done, including with object-oriented DBMS to help out.

Now with this in mind, we also have to remember that even though there are a ton of benefits that we are able to see when we are working with this kind of coding languages in our database, there are a few negatives that are going to show up and a few reasons why people may not want to work with this kind of language even on some of their database needs.

The first issue is that sometimes the SQL interface can be difficult to work with. Even though you do not need to know a ton of coding rules in order to start off with this language, it is still hard in some cases to interface with the database when you use SQL. This database is going to be a bit more complex in terms of its interface compared to just working with a few lines of code that we may find with some of the other options out there, so you at least need to take this issue into consideration.

Then there is also the issue that there are some features that come with this that are going to need third-party extensions on them. There are going to be some features that are added to SQL that will have to come with a third-party part in order to get them to work the way that you would like. If you do not want to take all of this effort to make it happen, then you may want to work with another language along the way instead.

SQL is going to be one of the best tools that you are able to use when it comes to handling some of the work that needs to be done with your database. It is a good method to use to store things to the database, make the tables that you want, bring in new information compare parts, bring other parts out, and so much more. When you are ready to work with your database and actually see some of the neat information that is inside, make sure to take a look at some of the different things that you are able to do with the SQL language.

Chapter 2: Some of the Basic Commands We Need to Know

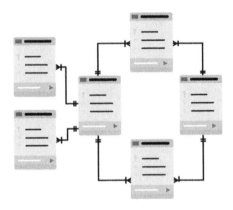

Now, before we are able to get too far into some of the codings that we are able to do with this kind of language, one of the first things that we need to learn a bit more about is some of the basic commands that come with this language, and how each of them is going to work. You will find that when you know some of the commands that come with any language, but especially with the SQL language, it will ensure that everything within the database is going to work the way that you would like.

As we go through this, you will find that the commands in SQL, just like the commands in any other language, are going to vary. Some are going to be easier to work with and some are going to be more of a challenge. But all of them are going to come into use when you would like to create some of your own queries and more in this language as well so it is worth our time to learn how this works.

When it comes to learning some of the basic commands that are available in SQL, you will be able to divide them into six categories and these are all going to be based on what you will be able to use them for within the system. Below are the six different categories of commands that you can use inside of SQL and they include the following.

Data Definition Language

The data definition language, or DDL, is an aspect inside of SQL that will allow you to generate objects in the database before arranging them the way that you would like. For example, you will be able to use this aspect of the system in order to add or delete objects in the database table. Some of the commands that you will be able to use with the DDL category include:

- Drop table
- Create a table
- Alter table
- Create an index
- Alter index
- Drop index
- Drop view

Data Manipulation Language

The idea of a DML, or data manipulation language, is one of the aspects of SQL that you will be able to use to help modify a bit of the information that is out there about objects that are inside of your database. This is going to make it so much easier to delete the objects, update the objects, or even to allow for something new to be inserted inside of the database that you are working with. You will find that this is one of the best ways to make sure that you add in some freedom to the work that you are doing, and will ensure that you are able to change up the information that is already there rather than adding to something new.

Data Query Language

Along with the same kinds of lines and thoughts here are the DQL or the data query language. This one is going to be kind of fun to work with because it is going to be one of the most powerful of the aspects that you are able to do with the SQL language you have. This is going to be even truer when you work with a modern database to help you get the work done.

When we work with this one, we will find that there is only really one command that we are able to choose from, and this is going to be the SELECT command. You are able to use this command to make sure that all of your queries are ran in the right way within your relational database. But if you want to ensure that you are getting results that are more detailed, it is possible to go through and add in some options or a special clause along with the SELECT command to make this easier.

Data Control Language

The DCL or the data control language is going to be a command that you are able to use when you would like to ensure you are maintaining some of the control that you need over the database, and when you would like to limit who is allowed to access that particular database, or parts of the database, at a given time. You will also find that the DCL idea is going to be used in a few situations to help generate the objects of the database related to who is going to have the necessary access to see the information that is found on that database.

This could include those who will have the right to distribute the necessary privileges of access when it comes to this data. This can be a good thing in order to use your business is dealing with a lot of sensitive information and you only want a few people to get ahold of it all the time. Some of the different commands that you may find useful to use when working with the DCL commands are going to include:

- Revoke
- Create synonym
- Alter password
- Grand

Data Administration Commands

When you choose to work with these commands, you will be able to analyze and also audit the operation that is in the database. In some instances, you will be able to assess the overall performance with the help of these commands. This is what makes these good commands to choose when you want to fix some of the bugs that are on the system and you want to get rid of them so that the database will continue to work properly. Some of the most common commands that are used for this type include:

Start audit

Stop audit

One thing to keep in mind with the database administration and the data administration are basically different things when you are on SQL. The database administration is going to be in charge of managing all of the databases, including the commands that you set out in SQL. This one is also a bit more specific to implementing SQL as well.

Transactional Control Commands

The final type of command that we are going to take a look at is going to be the transactional control commands. These are going to be some good commands that you are able to work within SQL if you would like to have the ability to keep track of as well as manage some of the different transactions that are going to show up in the database that you are working with.

If you sell some products online for your website, for example, you will need to work with the transactional control commands to help keep track of the different options that the user is going to look for, to keep track of the profits, and to help you to manage this kind of website so that you know what is going on with it all of the time. there are a few options that you are able to work with when it comes to these transactional control commands, and a few of the most important ones that we need to spend our time on will include:

- **Commit**—this one is going to save all the information that you have about the transactions inside the database.

- **Savepoint**—this is going to generate different points inside the groups of transactions. You should use this along with the Rollback command.
- **Rollback**—this is the command that you will use if you want to go through the database and undo one or more of the transactions.

- **Set transaction**—this is the command that will assign names to the transactions in your database. You can use it to help add in some organization to your database system.

All of the commands that we have spent some time discussing in this chapter are going to be important to some of the work that we want to get done and will ensure that we are going to find the specific results that we need out of our database. We will be able to spend some time looking through them in this book, but this can be a good introduction to show us what they mean, and how we will be able to use them for some of our needs later on.

Chapter 3: Creating Your SQL Tables

We have spent some time here looking at how to create a table in SQL. These tables are going to be there to hold onto the various types of data that we want to work with along the way. These tables are going to be able to make SQL work as efficiently as possible. What this means is that you are going to be in charge of creating the data that will go into these tables and SQL can make this easier than ever before.

There are a lot of times when we need to work with creating some of our own tables. We are not going to get very far with some of the databases that we want to create if we do not first work to create a few SQL tables These tables are going to help us to keep the information organized in the manner that we need and will make it easier for some of the searches that we would like to accomplish to happen.

You are able to create any of the tables that you would like, and these can hold onto all sorts of information. Maybe you have a table that is responsible for holding onto your products for sale, and then one that holds onto all of the customer information, and one that holds onto some of the information about the payments and transactions that will happen in your business.

You can then go through and bring up the table that you would like and then search for the information that comes in that table. If you want to look at adding a new product to your system, for example, you would be able to go to the product table and make the adjustments that are needed.

Depending on the kind of business that you are trying to run, and what you hope to get out of the process, you may find that there could be just a handful of tables to get the work done, and other times you will need to have quite a few of these tables to see the work be accomplished. You may need to go through ahead of time and figure out how many of these you are going to need before starting. This will help you to stay on track and will ensure that you are going to be able to get all of the ones set up that you want so nothing is going to get missing in the process.

You will not be able to get things to work as well as you would like if you do not add in these tables along the way. this is the best way to ensure that your information and your data is going to stay as organized as possible and that you are going to be able to get some of the results that you are looking for as well when you do a query and more.

The first step that we have to take here is to work with a new list, such as a shopping list, with all of the items that you want to work with found inside one of the tables in the database. We are going to start this off with a simple list to see how this is going to work, including three items, and the number of each item that you would like to work with as well. This will give us a good start to what we would like to see get done on this kind of process and will ensure that we are going to get the results that we want out of it.

The three items that we are going to work with to help us get the table created here is a blouse, underwear, and pants. We will have to go through and make a new command for the table that will then be able to store this particular type of list. So the sample list that you are going to see inside of the SQL that you are working with will look like the following:

/**Shopping list:

Blouse (4)

Pants (1)

Underwear (2)

**/

CREATE TABLE shopping_list(name TEXT):

If you place this syntax into the program, you are going to see that the table will have on the right-side column. You only listed that you wanted to have the text inside of the database, and nothing about the amount of the items, so the database at this point is just going to have the list of the things that you want to purchase (the blouse, pants, and underwear). Now it is time to add in the amount of each that you would like to have in the database. We need to add in the integer for this data type with the help of this new code:

/**Shopping list:

Blouse (4)

Pants (1)

Underwear (2)

**/

CREATE TABLE shopping_list(name TEXT, quantity INTEGER);

Now you will notice here is that when you look at the table, there is going to be a new column that will be listed out in the database that you worked with before. The first column is going to have all of the different items that you would like to purchase, and then he second one is going to have the amount of each of these items that you would like to purchase as well. This is going to be a nice way to create the table that you want to use because it will ensure that you are able to get the unique identifier that you would like to have for these rows, and can help you when it is time to delete or update the rows later on. If you are reliant on just using the rows for your identification purposes, you are going to find that this causes a mess because these values are things that can change for you later on.

After you have had some time to name the rows that you would like to have in the table, it is time to fill all of this in. You will find at this time that the table is not going to have any of the information inside that you would like, and you will need to use the command of INSERT INFO to help get this started. you will be able to set up the first column that you would like to use and then label it as 1, and then the second one is going to be a blouse, and then the third one is going to be how many are inside, which is four. You are able to continue on with this process until you make sure that all of the information that you would like to use is found in the database as well.

To make sure that all of these steps are going to be done in the proper manner, you will need to spend some time creating a good syntax. This will ensure that the table is going to look the way that you would like. The syntax, or an example of code, that you are able to use to help with that shopping list that we made a bit before, and will ensure that everything is in order in the code, will include the following.

/**Shopping list:

Blouse (4)

Pants (1)

Underwear (2)

**/

CREATE TABLE shopping_list(id INTEGER PRIMARY KEY, name TEXT, quantity INTEGER);

INSERT INTO shopping_list VALUES (1, "Blouse", 4);

INSERT INTO shopping_list VALUES (2, "Pants", 1);

INSERT INTO shopping_list VALUES (3, "Underwear", 2);

Once you have placed this information into your new table, you can take a look back at it any time during this process to see how it is going, make sure that the numbers are still the right way that you want. You can even change the numbers, delete some of the things that you are working on, and even add in some new items if you would like to expand the list.

There is so much that you are able to do when it comes to creating your own tables inside this program. While we just started out with a simple formula that has three items inside and a few items of each, you will find that most businesses are going to need tables that are much larger than this. You will still need to go through the same process in order to get this to work. Whether you just need five items or five hundred items inside of your table in order to keep all of your stuff inside the database, you will find that these same syntaxes are going to work, you will just need to use more of them.

As we can see with some of this, creating a table to work inside of the SQL program is going to be something that is fairly easy for us to work with. It is going to bring in a few different parts, and you do have the freedom of adding in the number of columns and rows that you would like in order to make sure that this database is going to work in the manner that you would like. You do have some freedom later on to make some of the necessary changes to your database, such as adding something new in, taking things out and more. There is a lot of freedom that is going to happen when you work with your own table in SQL, and it is one of the best ways to make sure that your data is safe and secure along the way, and that you will be able to pull it out and use it in the manner that you would like.

Chapter 4: Learning Phase One - The Basics

Now that we have been able to get this far, it is time for us to take a look at a few more of the basics that we need when it comes to learning with this language. We have looked at these a bit already, but now it is time for us to take a closer look at how to make it work, and some of the commands that are going to be important in this phase as well. Some of the different things that we need to explore when it comes to working with the SQL basics will include the following.

Extract Data - SELECT Statement

The first statement that we need to look at is the SELECT statement. This one is going to help us retrieve the items that we want out of the database. We can ask the language to bring back anything that we would like to view in the database, and the command that we need for this includes:

SELECT;

With this one, we need to go through and add in what we want to select. You can select a certain part out of a database or something from the computer that you are working with. But you start out with the SELECT keyword and go from there, telling it what you want to select. With this one, we will be able to gather up all of the records that are in that database and match up with our object that is named PC. However, the columns and rows of the result set are not ordered. To help us order the fields in the result set, they should be listed with a comma in the desired order that we would like to see after the command of SELECT:

SELECT price, speed, HD, ram, cd, model, code
FROM Pc;

When we take a look at the vertical projection of the PC table, we will find that we are also able to obtain this kind of listing when we use only the fields that are the most necessary to it. A good example of this is when we would like to be able to get the information out about the speed, and nothing else, of our processor, or the amount of RAM that our computer holds. We would then be able to work with the following code to make this happen.

SELECT speed, ram FROM PC;

Elimination of Duplicates - DISTINCT Clause

One thing that we are going to notice here is that the vertical selection that we would like to work with could contain duplicate rows on occasion if it does not contain a potential key ahead of time that will help us to identify the unique record that we want. In the PC table that we work with, the potential key is the code field, which is selected as the main key that we need for this table. Since this field will not be part of the query, the result that we get above has duplicate rows (for example, rows 1 and 3). If you want to get unique lines (say, we are only interested in various combinations when it comes to the processor speed, and memory size, and it will not necessarily be the characteristics of all the computers that are available and that you can use, then you would want to work with the following code:

SELECT DISTINCT speed, ram FROM Pc;

When we run this code, we are going to get the following output as a result

In addition to DISTINCT, the **ALL keyword** (all lines) can also be used, which is the default.

The ORDER BY Command

To sort the rows of the result set, you can sort by any specific amount of fields that you would like that was originally specified with the SELECT command or clause. To do this, use **the ORDER BY clause**. At the same time, *the field list* can contain both field names and their ordinal positions in the SELECT clause list.

This is going to be a good command that you are able to use when you want to make sure that you are not just getting some random order of information back at the time. instead, you want to put it in alphabetical or by the age of the data, to help you sort through that information and keep it as organized and easy to work with as possible. With this command, you can tell the database, and the SQL language how you would like things to play out when you are all done.

Sample - WHERE Clause

The horizontal selection is implemented **by the WHERE clause**, which is written after the FROM clause. In this case, only those rows from the record source will fall into the result set, for each of which the *predicate* value is TRUE. That is, the predicate is checked for each record.

Boolean Operators AND, OR, NOT and Three-Valued Logic - Predicates

Predicates are expressions that take on truth value. They can be either a single expression or any combination of an unlimited number of expressions constructed using the Boolean operators **AND, OR** or **NOT**. In addition, the **IS** SQL statement can be used in these combinations, as well as parentheses to specify the order in which operations are performed.

A SQL predicate can take one of three values: **TRUE** (true), **FALSE** (false), or **UNKNOWN** (unknown). The following predicates are an exception: **NULL** (no value), **EXISTS** (existence), **UNIQUE** (uniqueness), and **MATCH** (match), which cannot take the value UNKNOWN.

This can be a good way that we would want to go through and make sure that we are getting the right information out of the database that we are using. You would be able to use this to make sure that the data is only coming back as you would like.

We can take a look at the example of a search engine for this one. You do not want to have a bunch of items showing up that the customer does not want, especially if you have hundreds of items. You can use the Boolean operators to help you determine what items on the database match up to the query from the customer, and which ones do not, providing them with a seamless experience that will help them to get the most out of what you are providing in the website.

Comparison Queries

There are times when you will want to do a comparison between what is found on your database, and the query that you are completing. And maybe sometimes you would even like to go through and compare more than one part of the database to see what is all there. You could try to do this by hand or manually, but it will not take long before you find that, with a potential for millions of data points in the database, this is going to take a long time and be too hard to handle.

Instead, we can work with some of the comparison operators that are present in the SQL language. These will allow us to figure out if the different parts are equal, not equal, or something else. There are a number of these found inside of the SQL language, and this can really help us to find out what is there and whether it is going to work for our needs or not.

Chapter 5: A Look at Queries

While we have spent a little bit of time taking a look at some of the commands and queries that we are able to use when it comes to working in the SQL language, it is time for us to go more in-depth about these queries and what they are able to do for some of our needs along the way as well.

When we are working on our own business database and it is all set up the way that we would like, it is going to be possible that at one point or another you will want to do a search in order to make sure you are able to find the perfect information inside of all that. This is going to make it easier for us to find the easier information and results that we want. But we do have to make sure that the database is set up in the right manner so that we can use the right commands, and see that it is fast and accurate in the process.

Think of this like when someone comes to your website, searching for that particular product that they would like to purchase. Do you want them to get stuck on the website that is slow, and have them see results that have nothing to do with the item they wanted? Or would you like a fast search that was helpful and will encourage the person to make that purchase? Of course, for the success of your business, you are more likely to want the second option, and we can take a look at how to set up your database and work with queries in order to make this happen.

Working with the Queries

When you do set up the query that you would like to use, you will find that you are basically sending out an inquiry to the database that you already set up. You will find that there are a few methods to do this, but the SELECT command is going to be one of the best options to make this happen, and can instantly bring back the information that we need from there, based on our search.

For example, if you are working with a table that is going to hold onto all of the products that you offer for sale, then you would be able to use the command of SELECT in order to find the best selling products or ones that will meet another criterion that you have at that time. The request is going to be good on any of the information on the product that is stored in the database, and you will see that this is done pretty normally when we are talking about work in a relational database.

Working with the SELECT Command

Any time that you have a plan to go through and query your database, you will find that the command of SELECT is going to be the best option to make this happen. This command is important because it is going to be in charge of starting and then executing the queries that you would like to send out. in many cases, you will have to add something to the statement as just sending out SELECT is not going to help us to get some of the results that you want. You can choose the product that you would like to find along with the command, or even work with some of the features that show up as well.

Whenever you work with the SELECT command on one of your databases inside of the SQL language, you will find that there are four main keywords that we are able to focus on. These are going to be known as the four classes that we need to have present in order to make sure that we are able to complete the command that we want and see some good results. These four commands are going to include:

- **SELECT**—this command will be combined with the FROM command in order to obtain the necessary data in a format that is readable and organized. You will use this to help determine the data that is going to show up. The SELECT clause is going to introduce the columns that you would like to see out of the search results and then you can use the FROM in order to find the exact point that you need.

- **FROM**—the SELECT and the FROM commands often go together. It is mandatory because it takes your search from everything in the database, down to just the things that you would like. You will need to have at least one FROM clause for this to work. A good syntax that would use both the SELECT and the FROM properly includes:

- o SELEC [* | ALL | DISTINCT COLUMN1, COLUMN2]

- o FROM TABLE1 [, TABLE2];

- **WHERE**—this is what you will use when there are multiple conditions within the clause. For example, it is the element in the query that will display the selective data after the user puts in the information that they want to find. If you are using this feature, the right conditions to have along with it are the AND and OR operators. The syntax that you should use for the WHERE command includes:

- o SELEC [* | ALL | DISTINCT COLUMN1, COLUMN2]

- o FROM TABLE1 [, TABLE2];

- o WHERE [CONDITION1 | EXPRESSION 1]

- o [AND CONDITION2 | EXPRESSION 2]

- **ORDER BY**—you are able to use this clause in order to arrange the output of your query. The server will be able to decide the order and the format that the different information comes up for the user after they do their basic query. The default for this query is going to be organizing the output going from A to Z, but you can make changes that you would like. The syntax that you can use for this will be the same as the one above, but add in the following line at the end:

- ○ ORDER BY COLUMN 1 | INTEGER [ASC/DESC]

You will quickly see that all of these are helpful and you can easily use them instead of the SELECT command if you would like. They can sometimes pull out the information that you need from the database you are working in a more efficient manner than you will see with just the SELECT command. But there are going to be many times when you will find that the SELECT command will be plenty to help you get things done when it is time to search your database as well.

A Look at Case Sensitivity

Unlike some of the other coding languages that are out there and that you may be tempted to use on your database searches, you may find that the case sensitivity in SQL is not going to be as important as it is in some of those other ones. You are able to use uppercase or lowercase words as you would like, and you can use either typing of the word and still get the part that you need out of the database. It is even possible for us to go through and enter in some clauses and statements in uppercase or lowercase, without having to worry too much about how these commands are going to work for our needs.

However, there are a few exceptions to this, which means there are going to be times when we need to worry about the case sensitivity that is going to show up in this language a bit more than we may want to. One of the main times for this is when we are looking at the data objects. For the most part, the data that you are storing should be done with uppercase letters. This is going to be helpful because it ensures that there is some consistency in the work that you are doing and can make it easier for us to get the results that we want.

For example, you could run into some issues down the road if one of the users is going through the database and typing in JOHN, but then the next person is typing in John, and then the third person is going through and typing in john to get the results. If you make sure that there is some consistency present, you will find that it is easier for all of the users to get the information that they want, and then you can make sure that you are able to provide the relevant information back when it is all done.

In this case, working with letters in uppercase is often one of the easiest ways to work with this because it is going to make it easier and the user is going to see that this is the norm in order options as well. If you choose to not go with uppercase in this, then you should try to find some other method that is going to keep the consistency that you are looking for during the whole thing. This allows the user a chance to figure out what you are doing, and will help them to find what they need with what is inside of their queries.

As you go through this, you may notice that these queries and transactions that you are able to create for the database that you are working on are going to be important to the whole system and ensuring that it is actually going to work in the manner that you would like. In the beginning, this may feel like a lot of busywork to keep up with and that it is not worth your time or energy to do or that it is not that big of a deal. We may assume that with a good query from the user, they will be able to find all of the information that they need in no time.

However, it will not take long working with the SQL language and more to figure out that this is going to make everyone a bit frustrated. It is always better to go through and set up a good search query with SQL and make sure that your data is organized and ready to go so that everyone is able to find what they would like out of the database each time. This is going to be one of the best ways to ensure that you are going to provide the user with a good experience on your website, so take some extra care when you are working with this.

There are then going to be some times when the user is going to be able to do their searching and look up some information just by doing a search and finding the information that they want to use inside of that particular database. This is when they will want to ensure that the database is set up in a manner so that they are going to find the task or the item that they want right away, rather than having to continue to search and not having to put in many keywords in order to hopefully find the thing that they want along the way.

No matter which method you choose to use, or what seems to work best for the work that you are trying to accomplish with all of this, you will find that it is very important along the way that your commands fall in the right place each time and that they will lead you to the place where you want to be in your database. When you make sure that the table is going to be set up in the right manner so that you, as well as any potential users, are able to find what they want quickly and efficiently, you will find that it is so much easier to enhance the experience and grow your business.

This chapter is important because it shows us how to get all of this done. It helped us to see what was going on in the database and provided us with the right commands in order to bring out that information and make it work for some of our needs as well. While the SELECT command is often the one that is used to help control the database and make it work well, and you can choose the one that you would like to use. Setting up the database in a good and strong manner, and being careful with the commands that you are using is one of the best ways to ensure that you are going to get the best results with this along the way while providing your users and customers with the shopping and transaction experience that they want to enjoy it and that will get them to come back again.

Chapter 5: A Bit About Subqueries

The next topic that we are going to spend some time talking about is how to work with the subqueries in this language. We will take a look at some of the queries in another chapter in this guidebook, but getting a good look at what these subqueries are all about, and how we are able to add them into some of the codes that we are doing is going to be very important as well. Some of the things that we need to know when it comes to the subqueries in SQL will include:

More About Subqueries

Note that in general, a query returns a **plurality of** values. Therefore, using a subquery when you are working with a **WHERE clause** without **EXISTS**, **IN**, **ALL**, and **ANY** statements th at give a **Boolean** value can result in a query runtime error.

56

Example. Find PC models and prices, the cost of which exceeds the minimum cost of PC notebooks:

```
SELECT DISTINCT model, price
FROM PC
WHERE price
(SELECT MIN(price)
FROM Laptop);
```

You will find that this is the right way to work with this kind of request because the scalar value of the price is going to be compared back to the subquery that returns just one value to you.

The result that you will get with this is going to depend on what you are doing, but in this option, we will find that we will get the results of three models of PC's because that is how we worked on the code. You can input this into your SQL language and see what results you get.

On the other hand, a subquery that returns multiple rows and contains multiple columns can naturally be used in **the FROM clause**. This allows you to limit the set of columns and / or rows when performing the join operation of tables.

In addition, you will find that some of these subqueries are going to be found in the SELECT clause. This is going to make it possible to formulate a query very compactly.

We can take some time to look at how this is done. For this example, we want to be able to find the difference between the average price o a notebook PC, and the PC that we want.

Or, we would want to figure out, on average, whether the notebook is going to be more expensive than we will see with the regular PC. A good code that we can use for this will be the following:

```
SELECT (SELECT AVG(price)
FROM Laptop) -
(SELECT AVG(price)
FROM PC) AS dif_price;
```

Type Conversion

In implementations of the SQL language, implicit type conversion can be performed. So, for example, in T-SQL, when comparing or combining values of the **smallest** and **int** types, data of the **smallint** type **is** implicitly converted to the **int** type. Details on explicit and implicit type conversion in MS SQL Server can be found in BOL.

Example. Display the average price of notebook PCs with the preceding text "average price =".

Attempt to execute the request

```
SELECT 'average price = ' + AVG(price) FROM laptop;
```

will result in an error message. This message is going to tell us that we are trying to do what is known as an implicit conversion from the varchar data type over to money, and this is something that we are not allowed to do. This is because the system is not able to move one data type, especially this kind, over to another type, or a money type in this situation.

In these kinds of situations, the process of using an explicit type of conversion is going to help. If you end up in a situation with that error message from before, you can then choose to work with the CONVERT function instead. But we have to remember that even with this, the function you are working with will not be standardized. Therefore, for portability purposes, it is recommended that you use the standard **CAST** expression.

We can go through and make this a little bit easier to see. If we go through and rewrite the request that we want to use, working with the form below:

```
SELECT 'average price = ' + CAST(AVG(price) AS CHAR(15)) FROM laptop;
```

We will find that it is a lot easier to go through and get the results that we would like. The answer that you get here is going to be that the average price is $1410.44, but this number can change based on the input that we get, or what you are hoping to do with this kind of code.

We used an explicit **CAST** type conversion expression to cast the average price to a string representation. The syntax of the **CAST** expression is very simple:

CAST (AS)

It should be borne in mind, firstly, that not any type of conversions are possible (the standard contains a table of valid data type conversions). Secondly, the result of the **CAST** function for an expression value of NULL will also be NULL.

We can also take some time to look at another example of how this is going to work to our advantage as well. In this one, we are going to use the same idea in order to figure out the average year that certain ships were launched, working with the Ships table that we are going to work with here. The command that we want to use in order to make this happen includes:

SELECT AVG(launched) FROM ships;

This one is going to give us the result of 1926. In principle, everything is correct, because as a result, we received what we asked - YEAR. However, if you take a look at this, the actual mean of all the years does not quite end up with the same year as above. There are a few decimal points behind it. It should be something that we note that the aggregate functions we are working with, outside of the COUNT function that will provide us with an integer all of the time), will inherit the type of data that is in the possessed values.

Since we went through this and launched a field that was an integer, we are going to end up with an average value. And since the integer is usually not going to have a fraction of a decimal with it, we are going to discard this part of the year to keep things as simple as possible.

And if we are interested in the result with a given accuracy, say, up to two decimal places? Applying the **CAST** expression to the average will not do anything for the above reason. Really, this will:

SELECT CAST(AVG(launched) AS NUMERIC(6,2)) FROM ships;

...return the value 1926.00. Therefore, **CAST** needs to be something that we are going to apply to the argument that we will get with one of these aggregate functions. The coding that we can use for this one will be below:

SELECT AVG(CAST(launched AS NUMERIC(6,2))) FROM ships;

The result is 1926.238095. Not that again. The reason is that when calculating the average, an implicit type conversion was performed. Let's take one more step:

SELECT CAST(AVG(CAST(launched AS NUMERIC(6,2))) AS NUMERIC(6,2)) FROM ships;

As a result, we get what we need - 1926.24. You can guess from here though that we don't want to figure out exactly how long that .24 is supposed to stand for, and it can be kind of a pain, so we want to make sure that makes it easier. This is where we are going to work with more of an implicit type of conversion. The commands that we are able to use to make this one happen includes:

SELECT CAST(AVG(launched*1.0) AS NUMERIC(6,2)) FROM ships;

In the option that we did above, you will see that we were relying on the implicit type of conversion to go with our integer argument to the exact type of number, and then we went through and multiplied it by a real unit. And finally, we were able to apply it to the explicit cast of the result type that would become our aggregate function here.

Similar type conversions can be performed using the **CONVERT** function:

SELECT CONVERT(NUMERIC(6,2),AVG(launched*1.0)) FROM ships;

This will help us to finish up the conversion that we would like to see with some of the work and will ensure that we are going to really make sure that all of this works in the manner that it should.

The **CONVERT** function has the following syntax:

CONVERT ([()], [,])

The main difference between The CAST function and the CONVERT function is that with the CONVERT function, we are able to do some formatting with our data when we want to change it to a character type, and we can even specify out the format when we want to do some reversing on this.

The different integer values that we see here are going to fall together with some of the formats that we need to make this work.

CASE Statement

Suppose you want to list all PC models that are in your store and you want to make sure that the prices are with them. If you are going through this and notice that the model is not available for sale, which means it is not in the PC table that we create, then instead of the price showing up here, a text that says something like "Not available" will show up. We are able to use SQL to work with SELECT DISTINCT and then find the right PC model that we want to work with.

In the result set, the missing price will be replaced by a NULL value: This happens if we are working with a set that will not provide us with the prices that we need for those PCs.

To replace NULL values with the desired text, you can use the **CASE** statement:

SELECT DISTINCT product. model,

CASE WHEN price IS NULL THEN 'Нет в наличии' ELSE CAST(price AS CHAR(20)) END price
FROM product LEFT JOIN pc c ON product.model=c.model
WHERE product.type='pc'

The **CASE** statement, based on the conditions that you decide to specify, can return to us one of many possible values. In our example, the condition is a check the whole thing or NULL. If you meet with this condition, then the text of "Out of stock" is returned; otherwise (**ELSE**), the price value is returned. There is one fundamental point. Since the result of the **SELECT statement is** always a table, ten each of the values that we see in that column must fall into the same type of data (taking into account the implicit type conversion). Therefore, we cannot, along with the price (numerical type), derive a symbolic constant. This is why type conversion is applied to the price field to bring its values to a symbolic representation. As a result, we get:

We have to make sure that any time we use the WHEN statement they fall in the same kind of format, i.e. You cannot mix the first and second forms. When we start with the first form, then the command of WHEN is going to be done as soon as the value that is being tested in our expression turns to something that is equal to the value of any specified expression in that clause.

But if we move it around and work with the second from here, then this command is only going to b satisfied when you can get the predicate to be TRUE. When any of the conditions are satisfied as above, then we can bring out the statement of CASE, which is then going to return to us the value that goes with the clause of THEN that comes back to it. If none of the WHEN conditions if it fails, then the value specified in the **ELSE clause** will be used. If there is no **ELSE**, a NULL value will be returned. If several conditions are satisfied, the value of the **THEN** clause of the first of them will be returned.

In the code that we worked on above, we spend our time working with the second form of our CASE statement.

Note that to check for NULL, the standard offers a shorter form of the operator - **COALESCE**. This operator has a random amount of parameters that we are able to work with and it is going to be working to return to us the first non-NULL value that it finds.

Chapter 6: Transact-SQL Functions for Date / Time Processing

The standard that we are working with here is only going to specify the functions that we are using if they are able to return to us a system date and a system time together. For example, if we work with the function of CURRENT_TIMESTAMP, it is going to return to us both the time and the date of that together. Plus, there are also functions we can work with that will only return one thing to us.

Naturally, due to such limitations, language implementations expand the standard by adding functions that facilitate the work of users with data of this type. Here we look at date/time processing functions in T-SQL. The function that we are able to utilize to make this one happen is below:

DATEADD (datepart, number, date)

This function returns to us the datetime value, which is obtained by adding to the date the number of intervals that are going to be found in the datepart and it will be equal to the number we are looking at. For example, it is possible for us to go through and add in any number of hours, days, minutes, years and so on to the date that works the best for us. Valid values for the *datepart* argument *are* given below and are taken from BOL.

DATEDIFF Function

Syntax

DATEDIFF (*datepart, startdate, enddate*)

The interval that we work with here is something that we can measure out in different units. The options that we choose will be determined thanks to the datapart argument that we listed out above for the function of DATEADD.

One thing that we need to note here is that the time we are using for departure, which is the function of time_out, and the arrival time, which is going to be used with the function of time_in, will be stored in our Trip table under the type of datetime. This is a bit different if you are using any version that was before 2000 in SQL because these versions did not have the temporal types of data to get things done. For us, that means that only when we take the time and insert it into our field of datetime, then the time is going to be supplemented back to the date value that is the default.

Firstly, for flights that depart on one day and arrive on the next, the value calculated in this way will be incorrect. The second thing to consider here is that it is never reliable for us to make assumptions about the day we are on, which is going to be the present only due to the fact that it has to conform in some manner to our datetime type.

But how to determine that the plane landed the next day? This helps the description of the subject area, which says that the flight cannot last more than a day

But back to our example. Assuming that the departure/arrival time is a multiple of a minute, we can define it as the sum of hours and minutes. Since the date/time functions work with integer values, we reduce the result to the smallest interval - minutes. So, the departure time of flight 1123 in minutes:

SELECT DATEPART(hh, time_out)*60 + DATEPART(mi, time_out) FROM trip WHERE trip_no=1123

From there we are going to work on the arrival time and how we are able to use this for our needs. Some of the coding that we need to work with to show this will be below:

SELECT DATEPART(hh, time_in)*60 + DATEPART(mi, time_in) FROM trip WHERE trip_no=1123

When we get to this point, we need to be able to take a look at some of our times. We need to know whether the arrival time is going to be able to exceed the time of departure. If this does show to be true, then we need to subtract the second number that we have from the first so that we know how long the flight is. Otherwise, we will need to add one day to the difference to get this done.

Here, in order not to repeat long constructions in the CASE statement, a subquery is used. Of course, the result turned out to be rather cumbersome, but absolutely correct in the light of the comments made to this problem.

Example. Determine the date and time of departure of flight 1123.

The table of completed flights Pass_in_trip contains only the date of the flight, but not the time because, in accordance with the subject area, each flight can be operated just one time for the day. To help us figure out this kind of problem, we need to be able to add up some of the time that is in our table of Trip to the data that we stored in there as well.

Take some time to type in the code that we just did above, and see what the output should be. This should tell us a bit more about the time and so on within our output. If you type part of this in the wrong manner, you are going to end up with an error message so check that you write it all out the proper manner for the best results here.

DISTINCT is necessary here to exclude possible duplicates since the flight number and date are duplicated in this table that we are using for all of the passengers of the flight we are looking at.

Datename Function

Syntax

DATENAME (*datepart, date*)

This function returns the symbolic representation of the component, which is going to be known as the datepart, which is for our date that we specified before. The argument is going to spend some time specifying for us the date component and will tell us that the data is only able to take on one, and no more, of the values that are found on the table. This is going to give us a lot of chances to work with the process of concatenating the components of our data and getting it in the right format in order to present it to ourselves or to others.

It should be noted that this function detects difference values of *the dayofyear* or the argument tfor day when it comes to the datapart. The first of these is going to be more symbolic in the kind of representation that it is going to provide to the day when we go off the beginning of the year.

In some situations, we are going to notice that the function of DATEPART is going to be better served when we replace it with a function that is easier. This will often depend on what we are trying to do within some of the code we use.

All of these parts are going to be important in how we are able to handle some of the codes that we need along the way. Make sure that these are found in these types of codes to get the results you are looking for.

Chapter 7: Data Modification Operators

The DML that we are working within here, or the Data Manipulation Language, is going to come together with the statement of SELECT in order to get the right information from the database and then include other statements that change the state of the data. These operators are:

INSERT - Adding records (rows) to the database table

UPDATE - Updating data in a column of a table in our database.

DELETE - Delete some of the records that are found in the table of our database.

INSERT Statement

When we are talking about the statement for INSERT, we are looking at the command that is able to add in some new rows to any table that we are working with. When we take a look at our current cause, the values of the columns have the potential to be literal constants, but we can also see that they are just a subquery result in some cases. With the first situation, we will work with a separate statement of INSERT to insert each row. the second case, as many rows will be inserted as the number returned by the subquery.

Operator Syntax

INSERT INTO < *table name* [(< *column name* , ...)]

{VALUES (< *column value* , ...)}

| < *query expression*

| {DEFAULT VALUES};

As you can see from the syntax presented, a list of columns is optional. If this is a part that is not present in our work, then the list of all values that are inserted must be done. This means that the programmer needs to be able to provide for us the values for each column that shows up in the table.

When we look back at this particular case, the order that we see the values fall in need to correspond to the specific column order that the statement for CREATE TABLE said along the way.

In addition, each of these values has to come from the same type of data, and it needs to also be the same type that is defined in the column or columns that we chose with our statement for CREATE TABLE. This may not seem important now but it is going to make a difference in some of the coding that we are able to do with this.

It would seem that this is a completely redundant feature, which makes the design only more cumbersome. However, it becomes advantageous if the columns have default values. Consider the following table structure:

```
CREATE TABLE [product_D] (
[maker] [char] (1) NULL ,
[model] [varchar] (4) NULL ,
[type] [varchar] (7) NOT NULL DEFAULT 'PC' )
```

One thing to remember with this one is that the columns are going to come to us with default values. The first of the default values is going to be NULL< and then the last column is going to be a type of PC to keep it organized. With this in mind, we are able to write out the following to help us out:

```
INSERT INTO Product_D (model, maker) VALUES (1157, 'B');
```

When we look at this situation, the value that is missing when you insert one of these new rows is going to be replaced by the default value that is known as "PC" for this one. One thing to remember with this one is that if the value that is the default is not going to be specified for the statement of CREATE table and it is not a constraint of NOT NULL is specified that prohibits the use of NULL in this part of the table that we are working with, then we are able to assume that the value we are looking for on the default will be NULL.

The question arises: is it possible not to specify a list of columns and, nevertheless, use the default values? The answer is yes. To do this, instead of explicitly specifying a value, use the reserved word **DEFAULT**:

One thing that we can remember with this one is that when we would like to be able to insert a new row into one of our tables, the syntax is going to check all of the restrictions that are already imposed on that table. These could be unique constraints or primary key constraints. We can also work with the constraints for CHECK type to see if this is going to work for our needs.

Consider now the use of a subquery. Suppose we need to insert into the *Product_D* part of the table all of the rows that are found in our table of Products are going to relate back to different models of personal computers. Since these are going to hold onto the values that are needed to get started, the formation of inserted rows manually, firstly, is inefficient, and, secondly, it may allow input errors. Using a subquery solves these problems:

INSERT INTO Product_D SELECT * FROM Product WHERE type = 'PC';

The symbol that we used in this query is justified in this case, since the order of the columns is the same for all of the tables. If this were found to not be true, then the list of the column should be used to help us work with the statement of INSERT< or to do a subquery, and sometimes it can do it in both places, which would bring the order of the columns in correspondence:

There are often going to be a few other methods that we are able to work with here to get the same idea, and the option that you choose to go with will depend on the coding that you want to write, and what you hope to get out of the database.

While there are a few options that we are able to focus on here, keep in mind that the one above is going to be able to handle a lot of the work that you want to do, and will work just fine for most of the situations you end up within SQL.

Here, as before, you can specify not all columns if you want to use the available default values, for example:

INSERT INTO Product_D (maker, model)
SELECT maker, model FROM Product WHERE type = 'PC';

When we take a look at this cause, the default type is going to be found in all of the rows, which is then going to be the part that is substituted into the type of column in our table.

Note that when using a subquery containing a predicate, you will find that only the rows that we are inserting and will allow the predicate value of TRUE, rather than any that are UNKNOWN will be used. What this means is that if the table has the type of a column that is NULL in value, and this value was present in a number of rows, then these are going to be rows that would not be added to the table we are looking at.

To help us get rid of this restriction on taking in a single line in the **INSERT statement** when using **VALUES, the** artificial use of the subquery forming the line with the **UNION ALL** clause allows. It is possible to go through and write this out to meet our needs as well.

It is best to work with the statement of UNION ALL in this case, even if there are no duplicate rows, as in this case, a check will not be performed to eliminate duplicates.

Insert Rows into a Table Containing an Auto-Increment Field

Many commercial products allow the use of auto-incrementing columns in tables, i.e. fields whose value is generated in an automatic manner when we want to put in the new records. These types of columns are going to turn into the primary keys of the table because they automatically provide uniqueness.

A good example of this type of column is going to be known as a sequential counter. With this one, when you do go through and insert a row, it is going to generate out a value of one that is greater compared to the previous value. This previous value is going to be obtained when inserting the previous row.

An auto-incrementing field is defined using the **IDENTITY (1, 1)** construct. In this case, the first parameter of the **IDENTITY (1)** property determines which value starts the count, and the second - which step will be used to increment the value. Thus, in our example, the first inserted record will have a value of 1 in the *code* column, the second - 2, etc.

Since the value is generated automatically in the *code* field, the operator

INSERT INTO Printer_Inc VALUES (15, 3111, 'y', 'laser', 2599);

will lead to an error even if you are not working with any row that is in your table that relies on this kind of *code* field equal to 15. Therefore, to insert a row into the table, we simply will not indicate this field in the same way as in the case of using the default value, i.e.

INSERT INTO Printer_Inc (model, color, type, price) VALUES (3111, 'y', 'laser', 2599);

Because of this statement and what it can do, the information about the laser printer of model 3111, the cost of which is $ 2599, will be inserted into the *Printer_Inc* table. In the **code** field, there will be a value that can only happen to be equal to 15. In most cases, this is enough, because the value of the auto-incrementing field, as a rule, does not carry any information; the main thing is that it is unique.

However, there are times when you need to substitute a very specific value in the auto-incrementing field. For example, you need to transfer existing data to a newly created structure; however, this data is involved in a relationship that is just too many from that particular side. Because of this, we are not going to allow any of the arbitrariness on this one. In addition, though, we have to be careful because we do not want to abandon the auto-incrementing field because it will simplify data processing during the subsequent operation of the database.

Since the standard of the SQL language does not imply the presence of auto-incrementing fields, there is accordingly no single approach. Here we show how this is implemented in MS SQL Server.

Operator disables (ON value) or enables (OFF) the use of auto-increment. Therefore, to insert a line with the value 15 in the *code* field, you need to write

```
SET IDENTITY_INSERT Printer_Inc ON;
INSERT INTO Printer_Inc(code, model, color, type, price)
VALUES (15, 3111, 'y', 'laser', 2599);
```

Keep in mind here that it has to be written out exactly in the format that is above. If we do not do this in the proper manner, then we are going to end up with some problems in it, and we will get an error message in the code.

It is important to note that if the value 15 turns out to be the maximum in the *code* column, then the numbering will continue from the value 16. Naturally, if you enable auto-increment: **SET IDENTITY_INSERT Printer_Inc OFF.**

When we take a look at the auto-incrementing columns that we want to add in, there are a few things that we need to keep in mind. First, we need to take the last value that shows up in our code to be 16 here. When we are past this, then the line that has this value will be deleted out of it.

This brings up the question of what the value inside of this column is going to be when you are done inserting the new row? The answer is 17 here because the last value of our counter is going to still be there and preserved, even though we are deleting the line that is there at this time.

Therefore, the numbering of values as a result of deleting and adding rows will not be sequential. In addition to some of the other points, this is a good reason for us to insert a row with the missing, or the given, value in this column.

UPDATE Statement

There are going to be a number of times when we need to work with updating our table. If someone else is added to the database we work with, or we are trying to handle some changes to the table for our customers, for example, then handling the UPDATE command is one of the best ways to get this under control. The **UPDATE statement** modifies the data in the table. The command has the following syntax

UPDATE

SET {column name = {expression to calculate the column value

| Null

| DEFAULT}, ...}

[{WHERE}];

Using one operator, values can be set for any number of columns. However, in the same **UPDATE statement,** you can make changes to each column of the specified table only once. If there is no **WHERE clause,** all rows in the table will be updated.

If a column allows a NULL value, then it can be specified explicitly. In addition, you can replace the existing value with the default value that we want to work within our column.

If there is a reference to expression here, then we may find that this command is going to refer to all of the values that are currently in the table that is being edited.

It is also allowed to assign values of some columns to other columns. Suppose, for example, you want to replace hard drives of less than 10 GB in PC notebooks. In this case, the capacity of new disks should be half the amount of RAM available on these devices. This problem can be solved as follows:

UPDATE Laptop SET hd=ram/2 WHERE hd<10

Naturally, we are going to find that the types of data we use for the ram and the hd columns have to be compatible. If you want to help cast these types, then you would work with the command of CAST to get it done. If you would like to change the data based on the contents that we are seeing in the columns that you want to work with, then you would want to work with the statement of CASE.

If, say, you need to put 20 GB hard drives on PC notebooks with memory less than 128 MB and 40-gigabyte ones on other PC notebooks, then you can write this request:

You can also use subqueries to calculate column values. For example, you need to equip all PC notebooks with the fastest processors available. Then you can write:

UPDATE Laptop
SET speed = (SELECT MAX(speed) FROM Laptop)

In this case, the code will not be executed because the auto-incrementing field does not allow updates, and we will receive the corresponding error message. To accomplish this task nevertheless, one can proceed as follows.

In Transact-SQL, the **UPDATE** statement ng> extends the standard by using the optional FROM clause. This proposal specifies a table that provides the criteria for the update operation. Additional flexibility is provided by the use of table join operations.

An example. Let it be required to indicate "No PC" in the *Type* column for those PC models from the *Product* table for which there are no corresponding rows in the *PC* table.

This is a good way to ensure that we are able to join together a few of the different tables to each other. There are a lot of different methods that we are able to use to make this one work for us.

An external join is used here, as a result of which the *pc.model* column for PC models that are not in the *PC* table will contain a NULL value, which is used to identify the rows to be updated. Naturally, this problem has a solution in the "standard" version:

```
UPDATE Product
SET type='No PC'
WHERE type='pc' and model NOT IN (SELECT model
FROM PC)
```

DELETE Statement

This is a good statement to learn a little bit about. The statement of DELETE is going to b there to help us get rid of statements from any kind of table or cursor or even view that we want, and in a few of them, the operator's action extends to those base tables from which data was extracted to these views or cursors. The delete operator has a simple syntax:

DELETE FROM [WHERE];

If you are working with the WHERE command here, and it is missing, then all of your rows in the view or the table will be gone. This is true if the table is something we can update. You can also perform this operation (deleting all rows from a table) in Transact-SQL more quickly using the command

TRUNCATE TABLE

However, there are a number of differences in the implementation of the **TRUNCATE**

TABLE command compared to using the **DELETE statement**, which should be kept in mind:

1. It is not journalized to delete individual rows of a table. Only the release of pages that were busy with table data is written to the log.

2. Do not work out triggers. As a result, this command is not applicable if there is a foreign key reference to this table.

3. The counter value (IDENTITY) is reset to the initial value.

An example. You want to remove all notebooks with a screen size less than 12 inches from the *Laptop* table.

DELETE FROM Laptop
WHERE screen<12

All notebooks can be deleted using the operator.

DELETE FROM Laptop

or

FROM

Using a *table type source,* you can specify the data that is deleted from the table in the first FROM clause.

Using this clause, you can join tables, which logically replaces the use of subqueries in the WHERE clause to identify deleted rows.

Let us explain what was said by an example. Suppose you want to remove those PC models from the *Product* table for which there are no rows that would correspond to it in the PC table either.

When we stick with the syntax that is considered standard in this one, this is something that we are able to solve with the help of the DELETE FROM code if we would like.

An external join is used here, as a result of which the *pc.model* column for PC models that are not in the *PC* table will contain a NULL value, which is used to identify the rows to be deleted.

Chapter 8: Some More Learning Phases to Work With

We need to take some time now to look at some of more of the things that we are going to be able to do when it is time to handle the SQL that we want to work with. We need to take a look at the PL and SQL and how these are able to work with each other, and even how they are supposed to be different in some cases as well.

PL / SQL - "Procedural Language extensions to the Structured Query Language", which translates as "Procedural Language Extensions for SQL". Almost every enterprise-level DBMS has a programming language designed to expand the capabilities of SQL:

PL / SQL - in Oracle Database Server
Transact-SQL - in Microsoft SQL Server;
SQL PL - in IBM DB2;

PL / pgSQL - in PostgreSQL.

In these languages, programs are created that are stored directly in the databases and are executed by the DBMS, therefore they are called stored procedure languages. The languages of stored procedures have similar syntax and semantics, therefore, after mastering the PL / SQL language, it will later become quite easy to switch, for example,
to Transact-SQL or PL / pgSQL.

Function in Oracle PL / SQL
Function in PL / pgSQL PostgreSQL

```
CREATE FUNCTION F1 RETURN INT AS
BEGIN
FOR r IN (SELECT * FROM tab1) LOOP
UPDATE tab2 SET at3 = r.at2;
END LOOP;
RETURN 1;
END
CREATE FUNCTION F1 () RETURNS int AS '
Decare
r RECORD;
BEGIN
FOR r IN SELECT * FROM tab1 LOOP
UPDATE tab2 SET at3 = r.at2;
END LOOP;
RETURN 1;
END
'LANGUAGE plpgsql;
```

Tasks Solved by PL / SQL

PL / SQL, unlike Java, Python or C ++, is not used to develop mathematical applications, games, etc. It is a specific third-generation programming language designed to work with Oracle databases directly in the core of the Oracle server. In fact, PL / SQL programs are wrappers around SQL statements.

- PL / SQL is used to solve the following tasks:

- implementation of server-side business logic in the form of stored programs;

- automation of Oracle database administration tasks;

- web application development;

- development of client applications in the Oracle Developer environment.

We will not dwell on automating database administration tasks and developing client applications but focus on the main direction of using PL / SQL - implementing server-side business logic in the form of stored programs.

Use Case for PL / SQL Programs

Let there be an Oracle database in the corporate network on a Linux server with information about the organization's clients. Connect to the Oracle server from the laptop over the network using the SQL * Plus utility. Starting PL / SQL calc_clients_debt from SQL * Plus to calculate customer debt may look something like this:

```
SQL> BEGIN
2 calc_clients_debt (p_account_from => 100001,
p_account_to => 200000);
3 END;
four /

PL / SQL procedure successfully completed.
```

Only four lines to start the calc_clients_debt procedure will be transferred from the laptop to the Linux server, where the Oracle database server, having received these lines, will execute the PL / SQL procedure. Only information about the successful completion of the procedure will be returned to the laptop - one line. The gigabytes of financial data required for the calculations for a given range of 100,000 personal accounts will not be transferred to the laptop via the network - all client data will be sampled using SQL from PL / SQL and all calculations will be performed in PL / SQL by the Oracle database engine on a powerful Linux server. On the same server, in the same Oracle database, calc_clients_debt will also save the calculation results.

This is how a debt calculation might look if it were run by a technical specialist who knows the database device and prefers to work with it in SQL * Plus. It is clear that accounting or client department employees do not work with the database in SQL * Plus. For them, a client program in C #, Java or another programming language with screen forms and reports should be developed and installed. In this program, on the screen, the user sets the range of processed personal accounts and clicks the button "Calculate debt".

The client program, through the appropriate programming interfaces that are found in most modern programming languages, launches the calc_clients_debt stored procedure in Oracle and starts showing the user an hourglass or a running bar (progress bar) to the user. The program itself does not carry out data processing, which at this time is on a remote Linux server. As soon as the stored procedure successfully completes and the Oracle server reports this to the client program, it will give the user the message "Debt has been successfully calculated."

This is a typical PL / SQL usage scenario: implementing business logic (in this example, calculating customer debt) as a PL / SQL procedure stored in a database and running it from a client program that connects to an Oracle server via a network. Typically, PL / SQL programs run "under the hood" and are not visible from the outside.

Advantages and Disadvantages of Stored Programs

When implementing business logic, it is quite possible to do without using stored programs. So, the problem of calculating customer debt can be solved in two ways:

to develop one or several (frontend, backend) applications in Java, JavaScript, C ++, Python, etc., that implement only the user interface, and implement the business logic of the debt calculation itself in the form of a stored program that the applications call when the calculation process starts;

* to develop one or several (frontend, backend) applications in Java, JavaScript, C ++, Python, etc. that implement both the user interface and the business logic of debt calculation.

For the second method, the database is used only for storing data. All the necessary data for each client is retrieved by the application from the database, calculated by the application and the received debt information is saved back to the database. An application that reviews data is often placed on the same server as the database — so that the network does not become a system bottleneck.

The choice of the method used to solve the problem is the responsibility of the system architect, and many factors should be taken into account that is formed in each case based on the known advantages and disadvantages of using stored programs.

Advantages of Stored Programs

- portability of stored programs with the database;

- increased processing performance due to the lack of data transfer outside the database server;

- close integration with the SQL execution subsystem (SQL statements in stored programs are executed without the use of additional interfaces and drivers);

- control of access to data based on stored programs (access is not granted to database tables for reading and writing data to them, but to executing stored programs - thereby isolating data from application programs);

- implementation of dynamic integrity constraints and the concept of active databases using the trigger mechanism.

Disadvantages of Stored Programs

- "Smearing" the logic of the system according to several programs written in different languages;
- the need, along with Java, Python, C ++ programmers, to have a database programmer in the team;

- the scarcity of the expressive capabilities of the languages of stored procedures against the background of modern languages Java, Python, C ++;

- intolerance of stored programs between different DBMSs;

- possible problems with scaling.

The most significant drawback of stored programs is their binding to a specific DBMS. For example, when switching from Oracle to PostgreSQL within the framework of the current topic of import substitution, all stored programs will have to be rewritten from PL / SQL to PL / pgSQL, and this will lead to significant costs for reengineering PL / SQL code, which can amount to hundreds of thousands of lines.

As for the problems of scaling, the processing of data directly in the database using the DBMS itself is the advantage of stored programs until the required level of performance is provided. Otherwise, this circumstance will interfere with scaling, since the installation of additional servers will require a large amount of work. We will have to install a DBMS on each new server, create our own database with stored programs and solve the problem of distributing data across several databases. Of the virtues of stored programs, integrating data storage and processing can thus be a drawback. With separate applications that implement server-side business logic without stored programs, there is usually no scaling problem - adding new servers only for computing applications is usually quite easy.

Portability of PL / SQL Programs

Portability of PL / SQL programs along with the database is provided by the PL / SQL language architecture, similar to the Java language architecture.

When programming in C / C ++, Pascal, as a result of the compiler, an executable file is obtained. This file contains machine instructions for a specific hardware platform and is designed to work on a specific operating system. Therefore, if you copy the executable file for Windows to a computer with the Linux operating system, then it will not start there. If the executable file for one hardware platform is transferred to another platform (a computer with other machine instructions), then it will not start there either. As a result, if you need to provide cross-platform, then for the same C ++ program, you have to have a version for Windows and a version for Linux, a version for x86 (32-bit) and a version for x64 (64-bit) and so on.

The situation is different with Java programming. As a result of the Java compiler, the result is not an executable file with machine instructions, but a bytecode file - a low-level machine-independent code executed by a bytecode interpreter. This bytecode interpreter is called the Java Virtual Machine (JVM). When the Java program starts, a file with its bytecode is fed to the input of the Java virtual machine, which converts the bytecode instructions into machine codes of a specific platform. Thus, in order to run a program in Java in a particular environment, it is enough to have JVM for this environment. For example, in the core of the Oracle server, there is an Aurora JVM virtual machine designed to run Java programs stored in Oracle databases.

As a result of the PL / SQL compiler, the result is not an executable file, but a bytecode called p-code. This PL byte code is interpreted by the PL / SQL virtual machine (PL / SQL Virtual Machine, PVM) located in the Oracle database engine. There is a PL / SQL virtual machine in all versions of the Oracle DBMS for any operating system and for any hardware platform; therefore, PL / SQL programs remain operational when transferring Oracle databases from one computing system to another.

Evaluating PL / SQL

As a programming language, PL / SQL has the following advantages:

- static typing;

- availability of error handling tools and user exceptions;

- the presence of concise and convenient language constructs for executing sentences of the SQL language.

It is believed that efficient high-performance code for working with an Oracle database is easier to write in PL / SQL than in any other procedural programming language. In particular, in PL / SQL there are special means of bulk data processing (bulk processing), allowing to increase productivity by an order or more.

Here is a fairly large quote from the book "Oracle for Professionals" written by Tom Kyte, vice president of Oracle Corporation [18, p. 48]:

"When developing database software, I adhere to a fairly simple philosophy that has remained unchanged for many years:

Everything that is possible should be done in one SQL statement. Believe it or not, but it is almost always possible. Over time, this statement becomes even truer. SQL is a language with a lot of power.

If something cannot be done in one SQL statement, then it must be implemented in PL / SQL using as shortcode as possible. Follow the principle of "more code = more errors, less code = fewer errors".

If the problem cannot be solved using PL / SQL, we may find that working with the procedure stored as Java is the best to work with. However, after the release of Oracle 9i and subsequent versions, the need for this is very rare. PL / SQL is a full-fledged and popular third-generation programming language.

If the problem cannot be solved in Java, try writing an external procedure C. This is the approach most often used when you need to ensure the high speed of the application, or use an API from independent developers implemented in C.

If you cannot solve the problem using the external procedure C, seriously think about whether there is a need for it.

We will work with PL / SQL and its types of objects to help us work with our problems that are impossible or inefficient in SQL. PL / SQL is actually something that has been around for a number of years - it took more than 27 years to develop it (by 2015); in fact, back to Oracle 10g, the PL / SQL compiler on its own was rewritten a few times in order to make sure that it is as optimized for the work that it needs as possible.

No other language is so closely related to SQL and is not so optimized for interacting with SQL. Working with SQL in this kind of format is actually going to feel pretty natural, while it would be something that is hard in other kinds of languages that you would want to work with, and can be quite burdensome. "

The New Procedural Option - PL / SQL appeared in Oracle 6.0 in 1988. Since then, PL / SQL has written millions of lines of server-side business logic code and developed thousands of client forms and reports in the Oracle Developer environment. For many years, Oracle Corporation has demonstrated its commitment to PL / SQL, and with the release of each new version of Oracle Database Server, PL / SQL introduces new enhancements. PL / SQL is an integral part of Oracle technologies and the corporation plans to develop and support it in the future.

First PL / SQL Program

According to a long tradition dating back to C, textbooks on programming languages begin with the program "Hello, World!" And a description of the data types of the language being studied. We will not break this tradition, but make one change to it. Since the PL / SQL language is designed to work with Oracle databases, we will not set the string "Hello, World!" Statically in the source code, but take it from the database table.

```
CREATE TABLE hello_world_table (message VARCHAR2 (30));
INSERT INTO hello_world_table VALUES ('Hello, World!');
```

To make this a bit further, we are able to work with the following code, making sure that we do it in SQL Plus, to see what is going to happen.

```
SQL> SET SERVEROUTPUT ON
SQL> DECLARE
2 l_message VARCHAR2 (30);
3 BEGIN
4 SELECT message INTO l_message FROM hello_world_table;
5 DBMS_OUTPUT.PUT_LINE (l_message);
6 END;
```

7 /
Hello World!

PL / SQL procedure successfully completed.

In the PL / SQL program presented above, using the SELECT INTO command, the value of the message column of the hello_world_table table row is read from the database and assigned to the local variable l_message, the value of which is then displayed in the SQL * Plus window. The l_message variable is previously declared in the declarations section after the DECLARE keyword.

Screen output in PL / SQL is performed by the PUT_LINE procedure of the built-in DBMS_OUTPUT package, which is available in all Oracle databases. We can assume that DBMS_OUTPUT.PUT_LINE procedure in PL / SQL is an analog of the printf procedure in C.

Recall two things that are important when working with the SQL * Plus utility:

To run the PL / SQL program in SQL * Plus for execution, you need to type the / character on a new line and press the Enter key on the keyboard;

in SQL * Plus, the screen output of PL / SQL programs is enabled with the SET SERVEROUTPUT ON command (by default, screen output is turned off).

If you do not execute the SET SERVEROUTPUT ON command, then nothing will be printed in the SQL * Plus console. In the popular Quest SQL Navigator GUI client, the PL / SQL screen output is also turned off by default and is turned on by the special button "Turn the server output", which after pressing should remain in the "pressed" position.

PL / SQL Data Types

Recall that a data type (data tour) is a named set of data values of a given structure that satisfies the specified integrity constraints and allows the execution of a certain set of operations associated with this set. For example, numbers and dates can be added and subtracted, but strings and logical values cannot.

PL / SQL refers to languages with static typing. Static typing is called data type checking during program compilation. Static typed programming languages include Pascal, Java, C / C ++ / C #. Dynamic typing languages (JavaScript, Python, Ruby) perform most type checks at run time. Static typing can detect errors during compilation, which increases the reliability of programs.

Types of Data Types

Since PL / SQL is a procedural extension of SQL, PL / SQL has all the data types available in the Oracle SQL dialect with some minor differences. In addition to them, PL / SQL also has data types that are not available in Oracle SQL.

PL / SQL has scalar and composite data types:
* data of scalar types consist of one indivisible (atomic) value (logical values, numbers, dates, strings);

* composite type data consists of several values (records and collections).

Scalar PL / SQL Data Types

We also need to take a look at some of the types of data that we are able to work within this kind of language. The good news here is that a lot of the data types are going to look familiar, especially if you have worked with other coding languages in the past.

These types of data are nice to work with because they will provide us with information on what is going on inside of our codes, and what we are able to do with it as well. for example, if we are working with an integer data type, then we are handling a data type that works with numbers.

This is not the only type of data that we are able to handle though. It is possible to work not only with the integers, but with the characters, the varchars, floating numbers, and more. Pretty much any of the options that you will find in other coding languages will be found in this one as well.

It can be seen that the PL / SQL data types declared in the STANDARD package either correspond to Oracle SQL data types (_BASE types) or are entered as their subtypes.
Note the presence of the BOOLEAN data type, which is not available in Oracle SQL. Values of type BOOLEAN can, for example, be used in code of the following form:

l_amount_negative_flag BOOLEAN: = amount <0;
IF l_amount_negative_flag THEN ... END IF;

A significant difference between the PL / SQL and Oracle SQL data types is *the* greater maximum length of the values of the CHAR and VARCHAR2 types, designed to represent fixed and variable-length strings:

* for VARCHAR2 in PL / SQL, the maximum length of values is in the range from 1 to 32,767 bytes (in Oracle SQL up to version Oracle 12c, the maximum length of

VARCHAR2 was up to 4,000 bytes, in Oracle 12c it was also increased to 32,767 bytes);

* for CHAR in PL / SQL, the maximum length of values is in the range from 1 to 32,767 bytes (in Oracle SQL up to version Oracle 12c, the maximum length of CHAR was up to 2,000 bytes, in Oracle 12c it was also increased to 32,767 bytes).

PL / SQL Records

PL / SQL records are composite data types and are defined as sets of attributes associated with specific relationships. Record attributes can be either scalar data types or other composite types — other records and collections.

A PL / SQL record is declared as a user data type using the RECORD keyword, in general, working with PL / SQL records is similar to working with Pascal records or structures in C: If you have worked with this kind of coding language in the past, you should be fairly familiar with what we are able to do with these records and how we can pull them out for some of our own needs here as well.

Purpose of PL / SQL Records

* reading in the PL / SQL records the rows of the resulting SQL query samples (when declaring PL / SQL records based on tables and cursors using the% ROWTYPE attribute);

* combining several parameters of procedures and functions into one structure (instead of a large number of parameters of scalar types it is more convenient to transfer one parameter of a composite type to procedures and functions).

Compactness and extensibility of the source code is the main advantage of using PL / SQL records. Compare the two options for calling the procedure for printing information about a person - with one PL / SQL record parameter and with several parameters of scalar data types:

print (l_person) and print (l_name, l_secname, l_surname, l_born)

The first call option looks more compact. In addition, if it becomes necessary to process new information about a person, for example, TIN and SNILS, then for the second option, you will need to add two new parameters to all calls to the print procedure throughout the code. If you pass the description of the person in the form of a PL / SQL record, you only need to add new attributes to the declaration of type t_person. It is not necessary to make changes to the header of the print function and to its calls by the source code. By using PL / SQL records, this extends the extensibility of the source code.

Here are the basic rules for working with PL / SQL records:

* the definition of record attributes can specify NOT NULL constraints and set attribute values by default;

* assigning a record NULL assigns NULL to all its attributes;

* to compare two entries for equality or inequality, you need to consistently compare the values of all attributes in pairs.

Since PL / SQL records are similar to table rows, the advantages of using them for compactness and extensibility of the code are especially pronounced when executing SQL statements in PL / SQL. One row of the table - one PL / SQL record. Table rows "live" in the database, PL / SQL records "live" in programs. A row of a table can be considered as a single command in a PL / SQL record, a PL / SQL record can be inserted as a row in a single command, that is, data can be moved in both directions. PL / SQL also has special language constructs that allow you to move between the database and the PL / SQL program not individual PL / SQL records and table rows, but many of them. And all this is done very compactly - with one or two lines of PL / SQL code.

Bind Variable Declarations

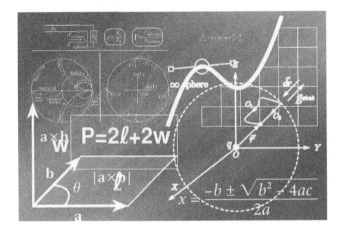

Since the PL / SQL language is designed to process the data that is in the tables of the Oracle database, it provides the ability to declare variables with reference to the schemes of these tables. For example, if some variable is used to read the values of the surname column of the person table into it, then it would be logical to indicate when declaring this variable a data type that matches the data type of the column.

There are two types of variable binding:
* scalar binding (using the% TYPE attribute, the variable is declared with the data type of the specified table column);

* binding to a record (using the% ROWTYPE attribute, a PL / SQL record variable is declared with attributes by the number of columns of the specified table or cursor).

Consider an example. Let the database have a table tab1 with at1 columns of type DATE and at2 of type VARCHAR2 (20). Then in the PL / SQL code, you can declare variables as follows:

```
l_tab1 tab1% ROWTYPE;
l_at1 tab1.at1% TYPE;
```

The variable l_tab1 will be a PL / SQL record with two attributes at1, at2, the data types of which will be the same as the data types of the columns at1, at2 of table tab1, that is, DATE and VARCHAR2 (20), respectively. The l_at1 variable will have a data type that is the same as the at1 column, that is, date.

Benefits of Declaring Bind Variables

* synchronization with table schemas is automatically performed;

* compact extensible code for reading rows of result sets of SQL queries without listing columns.

Automatic synchronization of variable declarations in PL / SQL programs and database table schemas makes PL / SQL programs resistant to possible future changes, such as adding, deleting or renaming table columns, changing their data types. In practice, such table schema changes occur quite often.

We give a concrete example. There was a client table in the CRM system database, in which there was an inn column. At the time of the development of the system, clients could only be legal entities with a TIN of 10 characters. Over time, the company began to serve individuals who have a TIN of 12 characters. The database administrator changed the data type of the inn column of the client's table from VARCHAR2 (10) to VARCHAR2 (12) and rows with long TINs began to appear in the table. Since in the PL / SQL code all the variables for working with the TIN were declared as VARCHAR2 (10), errors occurred when reading individuals from the TIN database in PL / SQL programs. If the variables for the TIN were declared in due time with reference to the inn column using the% TYPE attribute, then they would automatically "expand" themselves and there would be no errors at the execution stage.

Without listing the columns of the resulting SQL query samples, a very compact code is written like:

l_person person% ROWTYPE;
SELECT * INTO l_person FROM person WHERE id = 13243297;
print (l_person);

The SQL query selects all the columns of the person table, and the variable l_person declared with% ROWTYPE will have exactly the same attributes as the columns of the person table, with the same names and data types, in the same order. The values of all columns of the table row being read are assigned to the corresponding attributes of the PL /

SQL record. If a new column appears in the person table in the future, it will automatically be picked up by both the SQL query (SELECT *) and the declaration of the l_person variable in the PL / SQL program. No changes to the code will be required; the program will automatically recompile the first time it is accessed.

Variables can be declared as PL / SQL records using the% ROWTYPE attribute not only on the basis of a single table but also on the basis of columns of the resulting samples of arbitrary SQL queries. For this, PL / SQL records are declared based on explicit cursors.

Chapter 9: PL / SQL Program Structure

Now that we have had some time to take a closer look at the PL and SQL kind of structure from the last chapter, it is time to dive into this a bit more and see what else we are able to do with it. In particular, this chapter is going to explore some of the structure that comes with the PL and SQL program structure. Let's dive right in and see what it is all about.

Block Structure

In PL / SQL, as in most procedural programming languages, the smallest unit of source grouping is a block. It is a piece of code that defines the boundaries of code execution and the scope for ads. Blocks can be nested into each other.

PL / SQL Block Sections

A PL / SQL block consists of four sections:

- heading section;
- announcements section;
- executable section;
- exception handling section.

The heading sections, declarations, and exception handling may not be in the block; only the executable section is mandatory.

The syntax that we are able to find with this kind of process will be below:

heading section
Decare
ads section
BEGIN
executable section
EXCEPTION
exception handling section
END

The heading section indicates:
block type (procedure, function);
block name (name of the procedure, function);
parameter names, their data types and value transfer modes.

The declaration section declares custom data types, variables, and constants, which are then used in the executable section and the exception handling section. The executable section implements the actual program logic. In a degenerate case, there can be only one "empty" NULL command.

The BEGIN and END keywords in PL / SQL are operator brackets similar to the {and} characters in other programming languages and mark the beginning of an executable section and the end of a block. Each command in PL / SQL must end with a semicolon (symbol;).

Types of PL / SQL Blocks

There are two kinds of blocks in PL / SQL:
* named blocks (with header section);
* anonymous blocks (no header section).

Named blocks, in turn, also come in two forms:
* named blocks of programs stored in the database (procedures, functions, packages, and triggers);

* named blocks in the declaration sections of other blocks (anonymous or named).

Stored programs are objects of the Oracle database and are created by the CREATE DDL command, after which the named PL / SQL block is written. The block name indicated in the header section will be the name of the database object.

Anonymous blocks do not have a header section. If a block does not have a header section, then it does not have a name that is indicated in this section; therefore, such blocks are called anonymous.

Anonymous blocks are either embedded in other blocks or stored as text script files. In the latter case, anonymous blocks are usually used to call stored programs or to automate database administration tasks.

Anonymous block script file1.sql
- Anonymous nested blocks in a named block of a stored program

```
Decare
I INTEGER;
- named block of proc1 procedure
- in the anonymous block section
PROCEDURE proc1 IS
BEGIN
NULL
END
BEGIN
- proc1 procedure call
proc1;
END
- named block of proc2 procedure
```

Chapter 10: Other Things We Can Work On In SQL

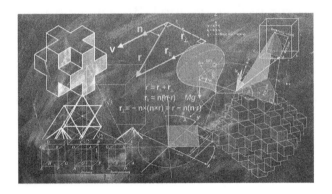

After we go through and do some of the initial loadings of some of the spatial columns that are there, it is time for us to go through and make a request, and then analyze them. MySQL provides a set of functions to perform a lot of the operations that we need when it comes to this kind of analysis. We are able to take these functions and then group them into four new categories based on what they are able to perform for us. These are going to include the following:

1. The first type is going to be the type of function that is able to convert a configuration between more than one type of format.
2. Then we have the type that is going to help provide us with the access that we need in order to work with quantitative or qualitative details that come with geometry.

3. The next type is going to be any of the functions that are going to help us get a description of a relationship between the configurations that you have.
4. Then the last kind is going to be the functions that are going to be able to create a new configuration from one that is already existing.

All of these are going to be important to some of the things that we are going to be able to do when it comes to spatial analysis. This kind of analysis can be used in a variety of contexts including:

1. Any kind of program in SQL that is interactive, including the SQL query browser.
2. Applications that are done in any other kind of coding language that you would like that are also able to support the client of MySQL API Geometry Conversion Functions.

Geometry Functions

Each of the functions that we are hoping to use in this and that will belong in a group will take the value of that geometry as a parameter, and then will be able to return some quantitative or qualitative property of the geometry that we work with. Some of the functions that you would want to work with along the way will end up limiting the types of parameters that you are able to work with. And these are going to provide us with a return known as NULL if the parameter does not provide us with the right type.

Depending on the information that we want to get out of our tables, we will find that these geometry functions, and some of the other options for arithmetic as well, will be useful to get the process done for us as well.

Property Limitations

While we are here, we need to spend some time taking a look at what is known as the property limitations when we work with the SQL language. This will ensure that we are going to be able to take advantage of what is available in some of our codings, and will make it easier for us to use with the database. Let's take a look at how we can make this work for our needs.

Views Limitations

View processing is not optimized: This will mean that it is unable to come in and create a new index on the view.

Indexes are helpful for working on the processed views because it will combine together more than one of the algorithms you want to work with at a time. However, we have to remember the view, which is going to be something we can process with a temptable algorithm, is not going to help us take advantage of the indexes on the tables that are considered on our main ones, even though w can use these when we want to make a temporary table.

Subqueries, on the other hand, can't be used if we work with the clause of FROM. This is going to b a restriction that will be moved later but is in place for now. There is also a good rule in place that makes it hard to modify a table and then do a subquery on that same table so keep this in mind.

The same principle also applies if you select from a view that selects from a table if the selection of view from a table in a subquery and view are evaluated using a combining algorithm. Example:

CREATE VIEW v1 AS SELECT * FROM t2 WHERE EXISTS (SELECT 1 FROM t1 WHERE

t1.a = t2.a);

UPDATE t1, v2 SET t1.a = 1 WHERE t1.b = v2.b;

If we find that the view is something that we are going to evaluate using an ability that is temporary, we are then able to select from the table in view with the help of a subquery and then change around that table with the help of a query that is external in the process.

If we end up doing this, then we are going to be able to create a temporary table to work with and then store our view in there for now. And we can really use this to make sure that we are not selecting from the table in the subquery and try to modify this table when we do not want to.

Along with this idea, we are able to force MySQL to do a few things here, including use the algorithm that we want. The right one to work with here is going to be the temptable one. This is done with the code of ALGORITHM = TEMPTABLE when we are in the definition of the view. From there, we are going to choose to either drop or alter the table based on whether we would like to modify or delete it. But keep in mind when we do this one, we are not going to get a warning at all.

The error that is going to show up when we try to do this will not appear until later when you actually use the view. The view definition is going to be frozen based on the instructions that are there. if the instructions were prepared with the command of PREPARE and it goes back and refers to the view, then the contents of this particular view are going to be the same any time that the execution happens.

This is going to be true even if you find that the definition of view is going to be changed once the statement is prepared, but this does have to be done before we execute that statement or it is not going to work. A good example of how we can do this is below:

```
CREATE VIEW v AS SELECT 1;
PREPARE s FROM 'SELECT * FROM v';
ALTER VIEW v AS SELECT 2;
EXECUTE s;
```

The result returned by the EXECUTE statement is 1, not 2.

If you see an instruction that is stored in what is a routine is able to access the view, then the content of the view is going to end up being exactly the same as what we found the first time we executed the instructions. For example, we can see that this will mean that if the statement is going to be done with the help of a loop, the further iterations are going to be in the same view content, even if you see that you will need to change up the view of the definition later on when you are doing the loop.

Regarding updatable views: the overall goal for a view is that if any view is theoretically updatable, it should be updatable and practical. This includes views that have a UNION in their definition. Currently, not all views that are theoretically updated are those in practice (maybe modified). The initial implementation of the view was intentionally written in this way to become usable; updated views in MySQL will be made fast as we are able to. When we have a lot of updated views on the database, it is possible for us to modify them and make changes, but we have to make sure that we know there are still some limitations that will exist on this.

If we are working with some of the subqueries that are present in our WHERE clause, then we know that we are working with ones that are updatable. But if we find that we are working with the subqueries that are found more in the SELECT list, this doesn't mean that we can't update those. Keep in mind here that we are not able to use the UPDATE command in order to work with more than one of these main tables at a time. We also can't go through and use the DELETE command in order to modify a view that has been previously defined as a union.

Along this same idea, if we have granted a user the basic privileges already in order to create a view in the database, then this means that the user is not going to have enough authority along the way in order to do the CREATE, SHOW, VIEW on that object unless you have given them that right along the way as well. This could lead to some problems when you try to copy the database. When you do not provide the user with the right authority to get it done, it is going to fail.

There is a workaround that we are able to use with this to get it to behave the way that we would like. For example, the administrator to manually grant these privileges if they would like to the users who have the authority to do CREATE VIEW.

In this though, we have to remember that there are going to be a few restrictions that we need to be careful about. The maximum tables that we are able to name in a single join will only be 61. This is going to also come up with the number of tables that can be named when we work with the view of definition.

Chapter 11: Data Security - What Could Go Wrong?

When it comes to the databases that you are using, you want to make sure that you are working with a format that is going to be as safe and secure as possible. Most of the databases that are out there are going to contain valuable information for a big company. They will hold onto the data that a company needs in order to get ahead, to help them keep track of their customers and more.

For example, it is not that uncommon for a company to go through and decide to work with a database to hold onto information about customers, and what they purchased at their store. This means that the company would have a lot of valuable information, including information on the individual's name, their address, their credit card information, and more. For a hacker or someone who would like to steal these identities, that is some really valuable information.

This is why, if you plan to have your own database along the way, you need to make sure that you actually take care of the data that you are working with, rather than taking advantage and assuming that it is all going to be safe. This is a wealth of information in your database, and certainly, a lot of other people outside of you would like to be able to get ahold of this information and use it for their own needs as well. If you are not careful with that information, then it is likely that they will, and this can cause you a loss of reputation and money, and really harm your customers

Now, there are going to be a few different types of security attacks that a hacker is able to do against your system, and you need to make sure that you take care of these along the way, and do your best to keep the network safe and secure as well. We are going to spend some time in this guidebook looking at some of the basics that come with this process, and explore how you can work to keep the database as safe and secure as possible.

SQL injection (also known as "Violation of the integrity of the structure of the SQL-query") is one of the vulnerabilities that we need to really take a look at when it comes to the security of our database is the SQL injections. These are so dangerous because they will allow the hacker to open up a back door into your network and system, and allow unlimited access: for example, delete tables, modify the database, and even gain access to the internal corporate network. An SQL injection is a pure software bug and has nothing to do with the hosting provider. So, you were looking for safe JSP hosting, PHP hosting, or any other, you should know that only developers, not the hosting provider, are responsible for the prevention of SQL injections.

Why do SQL Injections Happen?

SQL injections are a very common problem, but ironically, they are also easy to prevent. SQL injections are so widespread, since there are so many places where the vulnerability can be present, and if the injection is successful, the hacker can get a good reward (for example, full access to the database data).

The risk of SQL injection occurs whenever a programmer creates a dynamic query to the database containing user input. This means that there are two ways to prevent SQL injection:

• Do not use dynamic database queries.

• Do not use user data in queries.

Everything seems to be simple, but these are theories; in practice, it is impossible to refuse dynamic queries, as well as to exclude user data input. But this does not mean that it is impossible to avoid injections. There are some tricks and technical features of programming languages that will help prevent SQL injections.

How to Prevent an SQL Injection

Although the decision is highly dependent on the particular programming language, the general principles for preventing SQL injection are similar. Here are some examples of how this can be done:

1.) Don't Bring Out the SQL Queries All the Time

There are times when the dynamic query is going to be necessary. But for most cases, you will find that we are able to replace these with some stored procedures, parameterized queries, and even prepared statements. This can actually clean up some of the code that we are working with and will make it look a little bit nicer overall.

For example, rather than working with the dynamic SQL like you may feel needs to be done, you can use the PreparedStatement() in Java with some bound parameters to get it done. When working with the .NET platform, you are able to work with some of the parameterized queries, like SqlCommand or the OleDB Command() and then add in some of your own bound parameters to make it work.

Along with some of the prepared statements that we just talked about, it is also possible to work with stored procedures. Unlike the prepared procedures, these stored ones are going to be the type that you keep handy and stored up in the databases. But in both of these situations, the query from SQL is going to first help us to determine which parameters we should work within it.

2.) Validation of entered data in queries

Validating data entry is less efficient than parameterized queries and stored procedures, but if it is not possible to use parameterized queries and stored procedures, then it is better to validate the entered data - this is better than nothing. The exact syntax for user input validation is highly dependent on the database; read the docks on your specific database.

3.) Do not rely on Magic Quotes

Enabling the magic_quotes_gpc parameter can help us to sometimes prevent injections of SQL> The Magic Quotes is not the last defense and should not be treated as such, especially since they could be turned off without you knowing, or do not have the ability to turn it on. That is why it is necessary to use code that will escape quotation marks. Here's a piece of code suggested:

• Regular and timely installation of patches. Even when your code does not have vulnerabilities, there is a database server, server operating system, or developer utilities that may have vulnerabilities. That is why always install patches immediately after they appear, especially if it is a fix for SQL injections.

• Remove all functionality that you are not using.

The database server is a complex creation and has much more functionality than you require. And as far as security is concerned, here the principle "the more the better" does not work. For example, the extended system procedure xp_cmdshell in MS SQL gives access to the operating system, and this is just a dream for a hacker. That is why this function needs to be turned off, like any others, which makes it easy to abuse the functionality.

4.) Using automated tools for finding SQL injections

Even if the developers followed all the above rules to avoid dynamic queries with the substitution of unverified user data, you still need to confirm this with tests and checks. There are automated testing tools for detecting SQL injections, and there is no excuse for those who do not use these tools to verify procedures and queries.

One of the simple tools (and one of the more or less reliable) for detecting SQL injection is an extension for Firefox called SQL Inject Me. After installing this extension, the tool is available by right-clicking in the context menu, or from the menu Tools → Options.

You can choose which test to run, and with what parameters. At the end of the test, you will see a report on the test results.

As you can see, there are many solutions (and above all, all simple ones) that you can take to clear the code of potential vulnerabilities to SQL injections. Do not neglect these simple things, as you endanger not only your security but all the sites hosted on your host provider.

Conclusion

SQL Commands

SQL commands are divided into the following groups:

- **Data Definition Language Commands** - DDL (Data Definition Language). These **SQL** commands can be used to create, modify, and delete various database objects.
- **Data Management Language Commands** - DCL (Data Control Language). Using these **SQL** commands, you can control user access to the database and use specific data (tables, views, etc.).
- **Commands of the transaction management language** are TCL (Transaction Control Language). These **SQL** commands allow you to determine the outcome of a transaction.
- **Data Manipulation Language Commands** - DML (Data Manipulation Language). These **SQL** commands allow the user to move data to and from the database.

This guide, as you know now, is devoted to the study of Structured Query Language (SQL) and is complemented by a large number of examples that clearly demonstrate the capabilities of SQL. SQL is an ANSI standard, but there are a large number of versions of this query language. Whichever you choose, I wish you fun and success in your endeavor!

SQL

A 7-Day Crash Course to Quickly Learn Structured Query Language Programming, Database Management, and Server Administration for Absolute Beginners

hardships that may result from any of the information discussed herein.

Additionally, the information in the following pages is intended only for informational purposes and should thus be thought of as universal. As befitting its nature, it is presented without assurance regarding its prolonged validity or interim quality. Trademarks that are mentioned are done without written consent and can in no way be considered an endorsement from the trademark holder.

Introduction

Congratulations on purchasing *SQL Programming,* and thank you for doing so.

The following chapters will discuss all of the different things that you need to know in order to get started with the SQL language and to ensure that this is going to be something that you can use to really manage your database and get it to work for your needs. In this guidebook, we have spent some time splitting up the information and the tasks that you are able to do with SQL up into a week's worth of lessons, helping you to get some of the benefits that you need out of all this coding.

To start with, we will take a look at some of the basics that come with the SQL language. This includes some information on what SQL is all about, how the relational database is going to compare to the older, more traditional styles of databases out there, and some of the biggest components that we need to know when it comes to the SQL language. This will help us to get a good start when it is time to work with this language and will get us on the right track to success with these relational databases.

Then it is time for us to move on to some of the things that we need to know when it is time to handle the development of our database form the ground up. We will look at some of the components that show up in a database, some of the lifecycle of the system development, and how to build,

133

create, and delete the tables that are a big part of your database. We will finish off with a look at how we need to value and maintain some of the integrity of the data that is found in our database, as well.

On the next day, that is going to focus more on some of the different things that you need to do as the administrator of the database. These include things like setting up a maintenance plan for your database, so it stays safe and secures all of the time, how to handle the transaction logs, the best ways to do backup and recovery on the data, and so much more. Spending some time here is one of the best ways to ensure that your data stays safe all of the time, and will not start to get lost or corrupted.

Next on the list is taking a look at some of the simple queries that we are able to do with this language, as well. This means that it is time to dive into what a query is all about, how to handle some of the functions in your coding with SQL, how to work with expressions, and where the predicates and operators can add in some power to this as well.

The SQL server is another important part of this whole process, and we are going to spend a good deal of time learning what this server is and getting it all set up for some of our needs as well. We are going to learn how to add in the Oracle database, work with the SQL developer, and so much more. This ensures that all of the parts are going to come together for this database to work.

Then we are able to move on to the users and the roles. As someone who is in charge of running the database and setting things up, you also have to spend some time setting up the permissions and more of everyone who is allowed on your system. This chapter is going to be important because it can help us to log into the server that we have, assign the right roles to the right people in the database, and even shows us some of the commands that we need when it is time to handle these users and roles as well.

On the final day of this course, we are going to take a closer look at some of the tables and how they work in these databases, and how we can work with SQL in order to change some of the data that is found in these as well. There are times when you will want to create, add, delete, or change the data that is found in the different parts of the database, and this is exactly what we are going to spend some of our time discussing and working on in this chapter! This can really help to make the database into what we would like, and even though it may seem complicated, the SQL language is going to take some of the work and will ensure that it works the way that we would like.

There are a lot of times when we will want to work with a database to help our business to grow and to keep all of the data and information that we have that concerns our business in order. And the SQL language is going to ensure that we are able to make all of this happen for our needs. When you are ready to learn more about SQL and how this language can make the management and all of the other parts of running our database easier, make sure to read through this guidebook to help you get started.

There are plenty of books on this subject on the market, thanks again for choosing this one! We took every effort that we could to help us provide you with as much useful information as we could. We hope that you enjoy!

Day 1: Introducing SQL

Many companies are going to spend their time working with a database of some kind. We live in a world where technology and data are around us all of the time, and being able to use that data can make the difference in what results we are going to get overall in no time at all. It can help us to learn more about our customers, know how to reduce the waste that we are finding, and can make it easier for us to beat out the competition and provides us with a good way to make smart business decisions overall.

There are a lot of benefits when it comes to working with all of the data that is out there. But just gathering up the data is not going to be enough to help us get all of this work done. We also need to learn more about what this data means, how we are able to use it and to see some of the complex information that is there. When our database gets really big and has thousands, if not millions of points in it, we need to make sure that we have a good system in place that is going to help us to work with this language, and get the results that we are looking for all at once.

This is where the SQL language is going to come into play. There are other coding languages that are able to handle some of our needs when it comes to coding and looking through databases, but the SQL option is often one of the best ones that we are able to choose. We will find that this is a language that we can work with when we want to create the tables for our databases, put things together in our databases, and so much more. Let's examine some of the things that we are able to do when it comes to using these databases, and SQL for our own needs.

If you haven't worked with any kind of programming in the past, you will find that SQL is going to be a great option to help you get some of this work done in the process. The coding is simple, and even some of the longer codes that we need to focus on later will be straightforward and easy for us to learn how to work with.

Often you can look through some of the codes that are there and learn what they are saying, even before we actually go through and talk about them as much as we should. This makes it easier for us to gain some confidence in the coding that we want to do along the way, as well. With this in mind, let's dive into some of the work that we are able to do with the help of the SQL language, and see just how great this language can be for some of our needs as well.

A Look at SQL

The first thing that we need to take a look at here is what the SQL, or Structured Query Language, is going to be all about. This is going to be one of the standardized programming languages that will be used to help us manage some relational databases and carry out other operations on the data that is found in these. Initially, this was created in the 1970s, and it was used often to help database administrators but could also help developers when they were ready to write out scripts for data integration. It can also be used by those who are data analysts who want to be able to set up and then run some analytical queries as well.

There are a lot of ways that we are able to work with this language, including helping us to modify the table and index structures of a database, adding, updating, and deleting rows of data that is found in our database, and helping us to retrieve some of the information that we need out of the database to help with processing the transactions or to help with analyzing the data.

As we go through this language, we will find that the various things that we want to do with SQL, including queries and other operations, are going to turn into commands that are written out like statements. There are a lot of different options that we are able to use when it comes to these along the way, but some of the most common options are going to include SELECT, ADD, INSERT, DELETE, UPDATE, ALTER, TRUNCATE, CREATE.

SQL has become kind of the de facto standard programming language when it comes to relational databases after it showed up in the early 1980s. also known as the databases of SQL, these relational kinds of systems are going to comprise of a set of tables that will contain a lot of data that is in the form of rows and columns. Each of these columns in the table is responsible for corresponding back to a category of data, such as the name of a customer and their address, while each of the rows will hold onto the value of the data for that kind of column that you need.

Today, while there are other languages out there that are able to handle some of the work that we want to do in our databases and are able to make sure that we can gather up the information that we would like, it is important to note how well we are able to work with some of the SQL commands in order to get things done in no time. This is often the go-to language that we are able to use when it comes to SQL and getting our work accomplished in a database, and it is important to learn how to make this work for our needs as well.

What are Relational Databases

One thing to notice here is that when we talk about the SQL language, we are going to focus our attention on what is known as a relational database. This is going to be a set of tables that is formally described and from which we are able to access and even reassemble data in many different ways, without us having to actually go through and do any organization or changes to the tables that are found in the database.

The standard users, as well as the API that is going to be used in this, of one of these kinds of databases, is going to be the SQL that we talked about before. It will not take long before you are able to see how these statements are going to be used for both all of the information that is going to come off the database and some of the queries that are seen as interactive and then will help us to gather some of the reports about all of that data that we would like to work with.

The relational database is something that was originally invented in 1970. The idea that came with this one is that we needed to shift from storing data in a structure of the past, which was more navigational in structure, all the way over to helping us organize data in the manner that we do today, which includes organizing all of that data into a table with rows and columns that we need here. Each of the tables that we will work with, which is sometimes going to be known as a relation, in a relational database, it will contain least one of these categories of data inside of the attributes that helps keep it together.

To take this further, we are able to see each of the rows, which we can call by the name of a tuple or a record as well, is going to contain a completely unique instance of any kind of data that we are working with at the time. This is going to be known as the key to the database. You will find that these keys are going to go with the categories and will be defined based on the information. Each table is going to come with its own primary key that is pretty unique, to help us to identify the information that is found in that table. The relationship that we would like to see between the tables is something that we are able to set with the help of some foreign keys, such as one of the fields that are found in the table and hopefully we will be able to get it to link back to our primary key, and sometimes it is going to link us back over to one of the other tables that are found in our database as well.

To see a good example of this, we may find that one of these order databases for business would need to contain a database that helps us to keep track of our own customers. This one would include some information on the customer inside, including the address, the phone number, and name. Then we would have another table that is able to describe other information like the order, the customer, the data, the product, and the sales price of that item as well. A user of the relational database is going to be able to give us the view of a database so that we are able to find the information that we need for any purpose.

For example, if you are one of the branch office managers, you may decide that you would like to take a look at one of the reports that is found in the database, the one that will let us know how much customers are able to purchase a certain product within a date range. But it is possible to be in that same company but works in the financial part of the company, and will want to take the same tables in the same database, could get a report of all the accounts that still need to be paid.

We will find that when we work with creating one of these relational databases, we are able to go through and define all of the possible values domain with the help of the data column, along with some of the other constraints that we want to be able to apply over to that value. For example, it is possible to come up with one domain that is going to show us our future customers and then would hold ten names of these customers. But then we can constrain these to one of our tables, which would only allow us to go through and specify three of these names. Two constraints are going to be there in order to help us relate to the integrity of the data, along with the primary and the foreign keys as well.

While we are here, we need to spend a moment looking at a few key terms that we are able to work with along the path to making this kind of database work for our needs. These are going to include:

1. Entity integrity: This is the one that will make sure our primary keys in the table will be unique, and that

we will not have the value of this get set to null at any time.

2. Referential integrity: This is going to require from us that every value in a foreign key column is going to be found in our primary key from the table that it originated in from the first place.

Before we end on this topic, we need to spend some time looking at some of the examples of a relational database that we are able to work with. These kinds of databases are going to enable a user to manage some of the predefined relationships of the data through more than one database. Some of the popular examples of this kind of database would include things like the Oracle Database, Microsoft SQL Server, and more.

While there are many companies who are holding fast to some of the older types of databases that are out there, it is already being seen that these databases are not the right option for many at all. These databases are hard to work with, do not add in a lot of flexibility, and can make it hard to keep up with some of the work and technology that we are experiencing in our modern world. This technology is following us into all industries of the world, and it is so important to be able to find a database that will keep up and provide us with the results that we want for the success of our business.

This is where the relational database is going to come into play. We will find that when we are able to work with this kind of database, things are just going to get easier. We will be able to understand what is going on in the database. We will be able to explore what is in there, and really be able to pull up the information that we need. And as long as we set up the tables in the manner that we should, and focus on keeping the information safe and secure and upholding some of the integrity of the database along the way, we will find that it is so much easier to work with these relational databases more than any other kind.

Another added bonus to all of this is that the relational database is going to work with that SQL language that we are focusing on in this guidebook. And what could be better than focusing on this language and getting some of the results that we would like out of that in the process as well? SQL does the work that we want to accomplish with our database easier than ever before, and since SQL and relational databases work so well together, we are going to find that this is an added bonus to help us make our lives and our work easier.

New Databases vs. Old Databases

Most of the software products that we are going to work with today are going to help us to meet the compliances for both the relational database and some of the regular databases that are out there. this means that they are going to be able to manage both of these types of databases based on what you would like to accomplish. in today's market, you will find that a relational database is usually what people are talking about when they bring up the term database. But you will find that there are going to be some big differences when it comes to the way that data is stored between both of these systems.

One of the biggest differences that you will notice between the newer relational databases and the ones that were used in the past is how the relational database is going to be able to store all of its data in a more tabular form. This means that it is going to be arranged more in a table with rows and columns. But the database is going to store the data more as files. Some of the other differences that you may see when it comes to these databases will include:

1. You will find that a process known as database normalization is going to be present when we are working with the relational databases, but it is not going to be found in some of the more traditional forms of databases.

2. A relational database is going to support what is known as a distributed database. This is not something that is found in a more traditional database out there.

3. A relational database will find that the values of data will be stored in the tables, and then each of these tables will hold onto a primary key to help us pull it out and use it when needed. A traditional database will find that the data is going to be stored in either a navigational or a hierarchical kind of form.

4. Since we are going to store the data in tables when we work with a relational database, then the relationship between these values of data is going to be stored as well. Since the more traditional database is going to store the data more as files, then there is not going to be a relationship that happens between the tables or the values.

5. When we are inside of a relational database, the integrity constraints are going to be defined for the purpose of what is ACID. But a traditional database is not going to use this kind of security, or much security at all, to help us be protected against some data manipulation.

6. While this relational database is going to be there to help us work with a large amount of data and to let more than one user on at a time, a traditional database is instead designed to handle small amounts of data, and usually, only one or two users can get on it at a time.

One of the final and big distinctions that we are going to see here is that the storage of the data on a relational database is going to be more accessible. This means that the values are something that we are able to update in the system. And then, the data that is found inside of the RDBMS is going to be logically and physically independent at the time.

The Benefits of a Relational Database

There are some advantages that you will notice when it comes to these relational databases, and this is why a lot of programmers and businesses are going to rely on these kinds of databases to get their work done. One of the main perks of working with these relational databases is that they are going to make it more convenient for the users to go through and categorize and store the data that they want in an easy manner. They are then able to query the information later and filter it to extract some of the specific information for the reports that they would like.

The relational databases are going to be really easy for us to extend, and they are not going to be reliant on any specific information for the reports that you would like. After the creation of the original database, we will find that a new data category can be added without having to modify all of the applications that are already there in the process.

This is just one of the advantages that you are able to be able to see when you get started with these relational databases, though. Some of the other options that are available to you will include:

1. Accuracy: Data is going to be stored just one time in this kind of database, which is going to help eliminate an issue that shows up in other choices called data deduplication.

2. Flexibility: Some of the queries that may be considered more complex will end up being easier for users to carry out with this option.

3. Collaboration: It is possible for more than one user to get onto this database at the same time if they would like.

4. Trust: The models that are going to work with the relational database are going to be more mature and can be understood better than others, and this gains a lot of trust with the users.

5. Security: The data that fall within this kind of database can be limited so that only particular users are able to access them if this is what is best for your company.

SQL and the Relational Model

While we are here, we need to spend some time taking a look at the relational model. This is will be some of the conceptual basis of the relational database that we have been talking about so far in this guidebook. It was proposed by E.F Codd in 1969, and it is going to be a method of structuring our data with the help of relations. Remember that these are going to be some of the grid-like mathematical parts that are going to include the columns and rows of our system. Codd proposed this model for IBM at the time, but he did not know how vital and influential this work would become when it came to working on these relational databases later on.

It will not take long to find out that this relational model is going to borrow pretty heavily form things like mathematics, and it is going to work with a lot of the terms that are found in math like domains, ranges, and unions. You will find though that the conditions and the various features that it is going to describe are going to be easier to define when we use some of basic English that we are used to as well.

When we work with this relational model, we will find that all of the data has to be stored in relations, which are also known as tables, and then each of these relations will need to have a number of columns and rows in place. Each of the relations needs to have a body and a header as well. To start with, the header is just going to be a list of all of the columns that we will see in that table, and then the body is going to be all of the rows.

The second part that we are going to see with the relational model is going to be the usage of the keys. These are going to be specially designed columns within the relation, and they will be used to help us order data or relate data to some of the other tables within that database. One of the keys that is the most important here is the primary key, which is going to be used to help uniquely identify each row of the data that we have. to make querying for the data easier, most of the databases that are relational are going to spend some time and physically order the data in relation to the primary key as well.

In addition to helping us define how the data should be structured as we talked about above, the relational model is also going to set up some of the rules that we need to use to make sure that the data is held to a high level of integrity, which will be known as the integrity constraints. It is also going to define how the data should be changed up and manipulated. The model is going to help us to define the special features and the normalization to make sure that the data is stored in the manner that it should be.

Another thing that we have to consider here is how the SQL is going to fit in. basically, this language is able to provide us with some of the commands that we need to ensure that we can pull up, create, delete, and do other things within the relational database. It is a simple language that really only needs a few parts to be accomplished, but you will find that it is really going to come into play and will help us to get so much more done within our code in no time at all, and can make working with this database a breeze in the process.

The Major Components of SQL

The final thing that we need to take a look at here is some of the key components that are going to be found in our SQL. This one is going to be made up of about four primary components, and three of these are going to come with some acronyms for us to learn as well. Some of these are going to include the following:

1. A database engine. This is going to be part of our SQL that will help us to create and then drive the relational database that we are working with.
2. SSAS: This one is going to stand for the SQL Server Analysis Services, and it is going to be part of the data analysis component of all of this. If you are organizing a database in order to help you go through the data and learn more about it in the process, then this is the part that you need to spend some of your time on as well.
    a. This one is going to help us to create some OLAP cubes, which are going to be programming objects that are more sophisticated and can help us to organize the data that we have inside of this database. It is also useful for helping us to complete a process that is known as data mining, which means that we are going to pull out some of the relevant data from our database in response to the questions that we sent out.

3. SSRS: This one is going to stand for the SQL Server Reporting Service. It is going to be a component of this server that is going to provide us with some of the reporting that we need. It will be able to accomplish all of this, no matter what kind of operating system the database chooses to work with.

4. SSIS: This one is going to stand for the SQL Server Integration Services. This is going to be the part that will be responsible for doing the ETL or the Extract, Transform, and Load process. Basically, this is going to be a process that we are able to use in order to clean up and then format the raw data that we get from other sources so that it fits into and will work well with the database that we want to focus on.

There are a lot of times when we will want to work with the SQL system in order to get some of the great results that we are looking for. If you ever want to work with a database and are hoping to see some great results when it comes to this as well, then working with the SQL is going to make sure that you can accomplish all of this at any time that you would like. We will spend some more time exploring what we are able to do with the SQL language, and how important these databases are going to be for our needs, but we can find that this is a great starting place for us to know some of what is going to happen later on, and how we are able to use that for our needs as well.

Day 2: Database Development

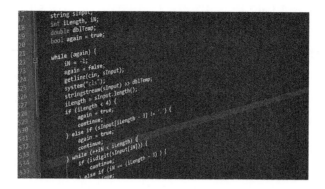

Now that we have had some time to take a look at what SQL is all about, and why we are going to see so much when it comes to working with the relational database, it is time for us to dive into some of the steps that we need to follow in order to start developing our own database as well. There are a lot of parts that need to come together to make this work for us, and we are going to explore those a bit more in this chapter, so let's get started.

The Components of a Database

The first thing that we need to spend our time taking a look at is the components that are going to be found in our database. The relational database is certainly going to be among the most common of these databases, and it is likely that you are going to spend a good deal of your time looking through this and figuring out how to use them. That is why we are going to start out our journey with a closer look at some of the components of this kind of table over some of the others.

First, we will see that there are some tables found in our database. The table is going to basically be the same thing as a record, which is going to be one of the fundamental components of the data. It is going to be comprised of a set of fields that are going to be the same in every record that you have, such as the name, address, and the product that the customer purchased.

This kind of database is also going to dictate how the tables are going to work. For example, this database is going to control how we are able to present this data onscreen and how we are able to organize the output that we have, based on what kind of query we use and more.

Then there will be the rows. You will find that the tables that come in this kind of database are going to look similar to what we see with a spreadsheet in Excel when we diagram them for a visual reference. The row on each of these tables will represent a sequential value where the value in row 1A, to start with, is going to relate to the values that will show up in all of the other fields that we use in row 1.

In addition to working with the rows, we are also going to see some use of the columns. These are going to be more of the control features, and they will show us a field of data that is going to occur in a consistent manner with each of the tables in our database. For example, you could have a column that has a header for address, name, email, and telephone. These are going to be the fields of data that we would like to have shown up for all of the records.

Primary keys are going to be the next thing that we need to work with as well. These are going to be kind of like the identification tags for all of the rows of data that you would like to work with. Each record is going to come with its own primary key in this kind of database, and it needs to be unique. The primary key could be something like a number that we have assigned over to the customer or be a unique kind of identifier, such as their SS number. These keys are important because they are going to be used as the queries within this database, but will not be used for some of the external databases at all.

And finally, we are going to end with the foreign keys. These are going to allow us to do some manipulation and searches of the data between the primary database table and some of the other databases that are related at the time. This can help to keep things more organized and allows us to find more of the information that we are looking for throughout more than one table at a time.

The Lifecycle of System Development

Now it is time for us to look at another topic that is going to be really important to what we can do with some of these databases, and this is more about the lifecycle that we will need to follow when it comes to developing our own system along the way. There is definitely going to be a cycle that we need to go through time and again in order to make sure that we are going to set up the database that we need, and get it to work, without having to worry about whether it is going to work the way that we want, and without having to waste a lot of time in the process.

You will find that there are a number of steps that we are able to take when it is time to work with this process, and if we are careful and go through each of them in the right manner, then our codes and our databases are going to work the way that we would like. Some of the steps that we need to follow when it is time to work on a system development project will include:

Planning. The first step here is going to be all about planning. In this step, we are going to spend some time discovering, identifying, and defining the scope that we would like to see with the project and then we are going to decide the course of action that we want to work with, hopefully to help us address the issues that we would like to be able to solve in this system solution.

This is a very important phase, and we need to spend some time with it because it is going to help set the tone for how successful we can be in this project overall. This is why, during this phase, we need to focus on doing a thorough amount of research to help us figure out the resources, budget, personnel, technical aspects, and more of the project that we want to handle.

Once we have had some time to take a look at the planning stage, it is time for us to work on the analysis. The purpose of working through this phase is to help us to better understand the business as well as the processing needs of our project at this time. In this stage, we are going to see that the development team is going to consider some of the functional requirements of the system to assess how the solution we are coming up with is going to help meet the expectations that are there for the end-user, right from the beginning.

We are able to figure out the requirements of our end-users, thanks to some of the research that we did before, and we are able to document these right away. Then we have to go through a feasibility study to help us to determine if the project is going to be feasible from a financial, organizational, social, or even a more technological standpoint along the way.

Now we are ready to go onto the third phase, which is going to be all about the design. After we have gone through and done a pretty comprehensive kind of analysis phase, it is time to work on the design phase. This one is going to take a look at the elements, components, security levels, modules, and more that we need to define for the system and then evaluate how we would like to see this finished system work for our needs, and even how it is going to look like in the end. This is going to need to be done in a lot of details to ensure that the system is going to include all of the necessary features to meet the operational and functional aspects of all projects.

Development is next on the list. We will find that an approved design phase from above is going to be important when we will work with the development of this system. When we reach this phase, we will find that our development team is going to be hard at work writing out the code and making sure that the system is going to get up and running. This one is often going to be the more robust of all the other ones because it is going to include all of the labor-intensive efforts and can help us to get the database done.

During this phase, we have to make sure that we test and work on the database a bit, as well. This ensures that we are positive that the data is going to stay in the database and that it is going to work the way that we would like in the process as well. We also need to go through and double-check that everything is safe and secure and that we, as well as the customers, are going to be able to rely on the database that we are creating in the process.

And finally, we need to spend some time working on the maintenance of our system. We can't just put a database up and hope that it is good forever on its own without any help from others or from some maintenance along the way. You have to take the time to check on the database all of the time, ensuring that we are going to see some of the results that we want and that no one will be able to get into the data and steal what they would like.

How to Build a Database

Now it is time for us to go through and do some of the fun stuff. We are going to spend some time looking at the simple steps that we are able to take in order to create one of our own databases in this process. It is actually easier to work on than you would think and can make a big difference in how safe and secure your own database is going to be in the process. Some of the steps that we need in order to create a database will include (we are using the SQL Server Management Studio from Microsoft to do this):

1. When we are in Object Explorer, we want to make sure that we are able to connect to the SQL Server Database Engine. Make sure to expand the said instance here.

2. Right-click on the part for Databases, and then click that you would like to make a New Database

3. When we are on that tab, we need t make sure that we are giving the database a good descriptive name that we will be able to remember.

4. To finish off this process of creating a database, we need to accept all of the values that are there by default. Then we can click on OK.

5. To change up the name of the owner, we can click on the three dots that are upon the top, and then select who can be the owner of this.

6. To help us go through and change up some of the default values of our primary data and transaction log files, we need to find our way to the grid for the Database Files, click on the right cell, and then add in the new value that we would like to use.

7. If you would like to go through and change up the collation of the database, we need to select the Options page, and then select the collation from that list.

8. We can also go through and change up things so that we are working with the recovery model. To make this happen, we need to end up on the Options page and select what is known as the recovered model from that list.

9. We can then move on and change up some of the database options if we would like. To do this, we need to click on the Options page, and then we can click to modify the options for the database in any manner that we would like.

10. To add in a new filegroup, if we would like, we can click on the Filegroups page. Then click Add, and then enter in the values that we would like to have for this.

11. We also have the option to go through and extend out a property so that it works with the database as well. To do this, we need to follow a few steps, but the first one is to select the Extended Properties page.
    a. When we see the Name column, we need to go through and enter the name for the property that we would like to extend.

    b. From there, we will need to take a look at the Value column. We can enter in the extended property text. For example, we could enter in one or more statements that we would like to use to describe the database that we are using.

12. And finally, we can create our database when all of this is done. We can click on OK to get this done.

There is one other method that we are able to work in order to help us create a database. If you are more into working with code and speeding up the process a little bit more, then this is the right one for you to work with. For this to happen, we are going to work with using the Transact-SQL. To make this happen, we need to work with the following steps:

1. First, we have to connect over to the database engine.
2. From the Standard bar that is there, we need to click on the tab for New Query.
3. We can then copy and past the following code that we will have into the query window that is there. when that is done, you can click on Execute to get it all finished:

```
USE master ;
GO
CREATE DATABASE Sales
ON
( NAME = Sales_dat,
    FILENAME = 'C:\Program Files\Microsoft SQL
Server\MSSQL13.MSSQLSERVER\MSSQL\DATA\saledat.
mdf',
    SIZE = 10,
    MAXSIZE = 50,
    FILEGROWTH = 5 )
LOG ON
```

(NAME = Sales_log,
    FILENAME = 'C:\Program Files\Microsoft SQL
Server\MSSQL13.MSSQLSERVER\MSSQL\DATA\salelog.l
df',
    SIZE = 5MB,
    MAXSIZE = 25MB,
    FILEGROWTH = 5MB) ;
GO

How to Create a Table

Now that we have been able to go through and create a
database of our own, it is time for us to go through and
actually create one of the tables that we are talking about
here. You will find that once the database is done and ready
to go, it is pretty easy to use a simple command in SQL in
order to create one of the tables. You can technically add in
as many of these tables to the database as you would need to
help keep your information nice and safe in the process. The
syntax that you are able to use when it is time to work with
creating the tables that you need in your new database will
include:

CREATE TABLE table_name (
    column1 datatype,
    column2 datatype,
    column3 datatype,
    ....
);

With this one, you will find that the parameters that we have
around the columns are going to help us to specify the

names of the columns that we have in this kind of table. Then we will also have the parameter for the data type that we want to work with, and this one is going to be important because it tells us the data type that we would like the column to hold. You can choose what kind of data you would like to place here, but it would be something like a date, an integer, or varchar, for example.

How to Delete Tables

We have now taken some time to see how we are able to create one of the tables that we need in our database. This is going to be useful when we need to sort through some of the data that we are using in SQL and want to make sure that it is all found in one place. Creating these tables is pretty easy, and you are able to use as many of these as you would like along the way.

With this in mind, we need to also take a quick look at how we are able to delete some of these tables. Over time, you may find that one of the tables that you are working with is going to not work the way that you would like, or maybe the information is outdated, and you would just like to clean it up and make it look a bit nicer without that table. This is definitely something that you are able to do with the right codes in place. The code that you will be able to use to make it easier to delete any of the tables that you would like in your database will include:

DELETE FROM *table_name* WHERE *condition*;

One thing to remember with this is that we need to be careful at any time that we want to be able to delete a record out of a table. We have to notice the WHERE clause as well as the DELETE statement. The WHERE clause is there to let the compiler know which of the records in specific you would like to see deleted. But if you do not add in this clause, you will find that all of the records of the table will be deleted. If that was your original goal, that is not a big deal, but it can make you lose a lot of information if you are not careful about what you are doing.

Checking the Integrity of a Database

Before we end with this chapter, we need to make sure that we are checking the integrity of our SQL database. This will ensure that the information is safe and secure and that all of the data that is coming in is going to be secure and will work the way that you would like.

There are a few reasons why you would like to make sure that you check out the integrity of this SQL database. Some of these are going to include:

1. If you find that one of the servers is running into some issues or has bugs in the environment and this is starting to go over to more than one of the servers of your SQL.

2. There is the potential for some inconsistencies between the server primary and log files and the database as well.

3. When you need to run some diagnostics to make sure that we are going to be able to check all of the integrity points of all the objects that are found in a specific database.

4. When we want to make sure that we are able to remove any of the corruption of our data that could potentially cause all sorts of issues inside of the database that we are working with.

5. Frequently when we end up with lots of statements in SQL that are failing, when we are not getting the results that we need that are correct, and when the instances are not working.

There are a number of methods that we are able to work with in order to maintain some of the integrity that we need with our database, but you will find that it takes some time, and you need to make sure that you are maintaining the right focus on the things that are needed. Always pay the most attention to the high priority kinds of databases, and then work your way down. This makes sure that the information that is the most important is going to end up getting the most attention in the process.

Day 3: Database Administration

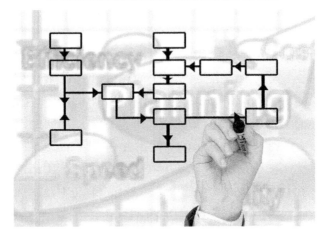

Now we need to take some time to look at some of the administration work that has to be done with any database that you would like to spend your time on. Those who are in charge of the database have to make sure that they are maintaining the database, that the information is correct and updated at the right times, and that only the right people are able to access the database and the information that is found on them. That is why we are going to spend a bit of time in this chapter looking more at some of the tasks of database administration and what we are able to do these work for our needs as well. Let's get started!

How to Set Up Your SQL Server Maintenance Plan

Making sure that you have an appropriate maintenance plan in place for some of the work that you would like to handle on the database is important. This will ensure that all of the information is going to stay safe and secure when it is time to work on your database, and will also help to add in some trust and more to some of the users who want to rely on that database as well. There are a few different steps and methods that we are able to use when it is time to set up our server maintenance plan. We are going to take a look at each one, but keep in mind that all of them work well, you just need to make sure that you are choosing the one that is right for you. And then make sure to stick with it for the long-term and keep up with it.

The first method that we are able to use for this is to help us create this kind of maintenance plan with the help of the maintenance plan wizard. The steps that we need to follow in order to get this done will include:

1. When you are inside of Object Explorer, we need to click on the little plus sign that is there to expand the server where you would like to have this plan.

2. Click on that sign so that you can expand out the management folder

3. Right-click on the fold for Maintenance Plan and then select on the part that says Maintenance Plan Wizard.

4. You can then go through the steps that are there in order to create your own plan for maintaining your database.

And then there is another option that we can use if you prefer, it will follow a pattern that is similar to what we see with the option that we had above. With this one, we are going to work with what is known as the design surface to get things done. This will include the following steps

1. When we are in the Object Explorer, we are able to click on the plus sign to help expand out the server where we would like to see this kind of plan.

2. You can then click on the plus sign that is there and get the Management folder to expand out.

3. While there, right-click so that you are on the Maintenance Plans folder. You can then navigate to the New Maintenance Plan.

4. Create the plan that you would like to follow, going through the prompts that come up.

The next option that we are going to spend some time on is using the Transact-SQL option. If you are fond of working with some coding to get all of this setup and to make sure that it is going to work the way that you would like, then this is going to be one of the best ways to get it done. To help you create your own maintenance plan with this option, we need to work with the following option:

1. When we are in the Object Explorer tab, we need to connect ourselves so that we are in an instance of the Database Engine.

2. On the Standard bar that we should see on this screen, click so that you are creating a New Query.

3. Copy and paste the ode that we have below and when it is done and set up nicely in the query window, make sure to click on Execute:

```
USE msdb;
GO
-- Adds a new job, executed by the SQL Server Agent service, called
"HistoryCleanupTask_1".
EXEC dbo.sp_add_job
  @job_name = N'HistoryCleanupTask_1',
  @enabled = 1,
  @description = N'Clean up old task history' ;
GO
-- Adds a job step for reorganizing all of the indexes in the
HumanResources.Employee table to the HistoryCleanupTask_1 job.
EXEC dbo.sp_add_jobstep
  @job_name = N'HistoryCleanupTask_1',
  @step_name = N'Reorganize all indexes on HumanResources.Employee table',
  @subsystem = N'TSQL',
  @command = N'USE AdventureWorks2012
GO
ALTER INDEX AK_Employee_LoginID ON HumanResources.Employee
REORGANIZE WITH ( LOB_COMPACTION = ON )
GO
USE AdventureWorks2012
GO
ALTER INDEX AK_Employee_NationalIDNumber ON
HumanResources.Employee REORGANIZE WITH ( LOB_COMPACTION = ON )
GO
USE AdventureWorks2012
```

```
GO
ALTER INDEX AK_Employee_rowguid ON HumanResources.Employee
REORGANIZE WITH ( LOB_COMPACTION = ON )
GO
USE AdventureWorks2012
GO
ALTER INDEX IX_Employee_OrganizationLevel_OrganizationNode ON
HumanResources.Employee REORGANIZE WITH ( LOB_COMPACTION = ON )
GO
USE AdventureWorks2012
GO
ALTER INDEX IX_Employee_OrganizationNode ON
HumanResources.Employee REORGANIZE WITH ( LOB_COMPACTION = ON )
GO
USE AdventureWorks2012
GO
ALTER INDEX PK_Employee_BusinessEntityID ON
HumanResources.Employee REORGANIZE WITH ( LOB  COMPACTION = ON )
GO
'
;
   @retry_attempts = 5,
   @retry_interval = 5 ;
GO
-- Creates a schedule named RunOnce that executes every day when the time on
the server is 23:00.
EXEC dbo.sp_add_schedule
   @schedule_name = N'RunOnce',
   @freq_type = 4,
   @freq_interval – 1,
   @active_start_time = 233000 ;
GO
-- Attaches the RunOnce schedule to the job HistoryCleanupTask_1.
EXEC sp_attach_schedule
   @job_name = N'HistoryCleanupTask_1',
   @schedule_name = N'RunOnce' ;
GO
```

This code is going to look a bit long, but it is going to be necessary to ensure that we are able to get the accurate results that we need, and for helping us to really make sure that the maintenance plan is set up and ready to go when we need it.

Backup and Recovery for Best Results

If you have a database, you need to go through the steps to make sure that you are backing up all of the data on a regular basis. There are things that can happen, even on a system that is working, and you really do not want to lose all of the information that is on the database. And if there is an outage, a mistake, a virus that gets on the computer or something else that could harm your database, you could find that you will lose it all, and have to start from scratch, if something like this goes on.

No matter how big or small your database is, you need to make sure that you work with some kind of backup plan. And it is often a good option to do this a few times. You should, along with your maintenance plan, have something in place that is going to help you to back up your information on a regular basis. The more often that you do this, the better.

There are a few options that we are able to use when it is time to back up our information on the database. There are some nice cloud-based options to work with. But working with some hardware is a good option as well because it ensures that you are not going to run into problems if something happens with that cloud-based service. If you would like to work with both of these, that can be a good option as well just to be extra safe.

Then, if the worst-case scenario does happen, you will be able to just go to the latest back up that you have, and hopefully it hasn't been too long since you last did it, and get the information back. It is hopeful that you have been using the right security measures so that this never has to happen. But just in case, having this organized is going to make a difference in how much of a headache the whole situation can be.

The Transaction Log

Next, we need to take a look at the transaction log. All of the SQL databases that you work with will come with a transaction log. This will hold onto all of the transactions and the modifications that happen to the database when each of the transactions between you and the customer happens. This is going to be a very important part of the database that you work with, and it is not something that you should skim over at all. If you find that at some point, you have a failure in the system, you would need to work with this log in order to bring this database back to where you need it.

One thing that we need to keep in mind is that we should not move or delete this log unless we fully know some of the ramifications that could happen when we do this. You can always use this kind of transaction log when you need to help recover your database to help make sure that all of the parts are going to head back where they belong.

There are a few different operations that we are able to support when we work with one of these transaction logs. Some of the most common options and the ones that you will be able to rely on quite a bit with your database will include:

1. Individual transaction recovery when you need that information back.
2. Recovery of all the transactions that are incomplete when the server is started up again. This could

include some of those that were in the cart, and the customer was deciding on at that time.

3. Rolling in a restored page, filegroup, file, or database, so it goes forward to the point of failure in many cases.

4. Supports the replication of the transactions that we have.

5. Supports high quality and strategies for disaster recovery. This can include some options like log shipping, database mirroring, and Always On availability groups if you would need them.

There are also a few different characteristics that we are going to see in this kind of transaction log. This is going to be something that can be implemented either on its own as a separate file, or you can have it come in as a set of files in the database. The log cache is going to be managed in a separated manner from the bugger cache that we see with the data pages, which is going to provide us with some code that is robust, fast, and simple.

The format that is going to log the records and pages is not going to have some of the same constraints as other parts of the code. This means that the log records will not have to follow the same kind of format that we see with the data pages unless we would like them to.

Next, we will find that we are able to implement the transaction log on more than one file. The files can be defined in a manner to expand out automatically when we go through and set the value of FILEGROWTH for the log. This is going to reduce the potential that we have when it comes to running out of space in our log while reducing the overhead that we have to deal with. The mechanism that we have to work with to reuse the space inside of this log file is going to be quick, and it is not going to have a big effect on the throughput of that particular transaction either.

Database Restores

Now, we all hope that we are able to start up with a new database, and it is all going to work nice and easy the way that we would like. But sometimes, we may find that it is hard to go through and get the database to work, and we will have to take a few steps to help us to back up the database that we have. before we are able to restore our database, though, with the full, or even the bulk-logged recovery model, you may need to spend some time backing up the active transaction log.

When you want to restore a database from another instance, you would have to consider a few things, such as figuring out how to manage your metadata when it is time to make a database available on another instance of a server. If you would like to go through and restore some of the encrypted types of databases, you have to make sure that you access the certificate or an asymmetric key that was originally used to encrypt the database. Without this, it is impossible to restore the database in the manner that we need. You need to retain the certificate used to help encrypt the database for as long as you would need to when it is time to save the backup.

It is even possible to go through and restore one of the older versions of a database in this server. When you do this, though, you will find that it is going to upgrade your SQL Server to the newest version. In this case, it would be the 2019 version. This is going to preclude the database from being used with one of the older versions of the database engine. This is going to relate more to the metadata upgrade, and it is not going to affect you when it comes to the compatibility level of the database. This means that it will keep the same kind of compatibility level when the upgrade is done.

Often you will find that the database is going to be available for you to use right away. However, if a Server 2005 database has the full-text indexes, the upgrade process will either import, reset, ore rebuild the indexes based on the choices that you made. If you then go through and set the option of the upgrade to Rebuild or Import, then these indexes will take some time and not be available during the upgrade. Depending on how much of the data you are trying to index, this could take a few hours to import and even longer to rebuild, so keep that in mind. It will get done, but it will take a bit of time to get that far.

When you set an upgrade option on one of these servers to import, and you are not working with an available full-text catalog, then the associated full-text indexes are going to be the one that we rebuild. This process does, however, take some time to finish, but it is going to be important to ensure that our database is going to work the way that we would like.

Recovery Models, You Can Use

And finally, we need to take a look at some of the different recovery models that we are able to choose from. The option that you work with is going to depend on what makes the most sense for your needs and what you would like to see happen with some of the work that you are doing on your database.

With the first option, we are going to work with the simple recovery model. The first thing that we need to remember about this is that there will not be any log backups. This one is automatically going to reclaim some of the log space so that the requirements that you have for this are going to stay small. This helps to keep some of the need that we have for managing the transaction log space that we have as well.

Operations that are going to require that their transaction lock backups are not going to be something that the simple recovery model is going to be able to handle. And there are a few other features that we are going to miss out on when we work with this kind of backup option. Some of these are going to include:

1. Log shipping
2. The mirroring of the database or Always On.
3. Media recovery without some kind of loss in the data.
4. Point-in-time restores.

We also have to take a look at some of the exposure that we have to lose our work. In this simple method, the changes since the latest backup are not going to be unprotected. This means that if there is some kind of disaster that shows up, you will need to go through and redo these changes along the way. This one is only able to recover to the end of the backup and nothing else. If you are working with a really large dataset or some sensitive information in this one, then you should go with one of the other options that are available.

The second option that we are going to work with is going to be the full backup. This one is going to require that we have some kind of log backup with it. No work is going to be lost due to damaged data files or files that are lost. It is also able to recover to a point in time that is arbitrary, such as the past error of the user or the past application that you would like to use.

In the full backup, your potential to lose the information is going to be pretty small. If the tail of our log does happen to get damaged in this, the changes since the most recent log backup have to be done over again, but since this is not going to happen all that much, you will not need to worry about this at all. One thing to note here is that if you are working with two or more full-recovery model databases that have to be logically consistent, then you need to be able to implement some of the special procedures to help make sure that you are able o recover on these databases.

And the third option that we are able to work with when it comes to recovering your data is the bulk-logged option. This one is also going to require a backup for the logs. It is going to be a kind of adjunct to the full recovery model that is going to allow us to handle copy operations of a bulk amount of information. This one is also good because it is going to reduce some of the usages of the log space using a minimum logging amount for these operations.

When you are working with the bulk-logged backup, you will find that the potential loss is not going to be that much. If you notice that the log is corrupted or some of the large-scale operations have taken place since the latest of these backups, sometimes the changes since that time need to be redone as well. Otherwise, you will not need to worry about the work being lost. You are also able to recover to the end of the backup that you do. You will find that the idea of a point in time recovery will not be supported in this.

Taking care of the database that you are working on is going to be so important if you want to make sure that it is going to behave in the manner that you want. Backing up the information, whether you do it with some of the methods above or not, is going to ensure that you don't lose things when the worst-case scenario does happen along the way.

Day 4: Working with Simple Queries in SQL

Now it is time for us to take a look at some of the great things that we are able to do when it is time to handle queries and more in our database. When your database starts to get really large, it is likely that you will want to spend some time searching for the information that you want. Without the help of a few commands to help you to get all of this done, you are going to end up with a bit of a problem along the way, as well. We are going to spend some time here taking a look at some of the ways that you can search through your database and some of the other commands that we need to know in order to help us to get things done in SQL in the database.

What is a Query?

A query of the database is going to be able to help us to take out information out of the database that we have, and then will be able to go through and format it into a form that is easier for us to read through and understand. A query needs to be written out in the syntax that a database requires. Each database is going t be a bit different, but you will find that many of them are going to work with the SQL that we are talking about here.

These SQL queries, with the help of a Data Manipulation Language, is going to come in with four different blocks. The first two are not going to be optional, so we need to make sure that they are there. These are going to tell the compiler what we are hoping to bring out and where it is going to be found. And often, this is going to include the SELECT command to help us get it all done. At the most basic form, we will find that the SQL query is going to look like the following:

SELECT X from Y;

In this one, the SELECT keyword is going to help us identify what information we would like to display out of the database, and then the FROM keyword is going to help us to identify where the data is going to come from and how these data sources are going to associate with each other.

There are some optional points that we are able to see with this one, as well. We can work with the WHERE command if we would like to set up some criteria that limit the search a little bit. Then there is the ORDER BY and the GROUP BY statements that are going to help us to associate the values that we need and go through and display them in the sequence that is needed the most.

Bringing in the Functions

The next thing that we will need to spend some time on is the functions that show up in our database. These functions are important because they are going to help us perform various actions on the database that we are working with. For the most part, we are going to spend our time working with the four main types of database functions because these are the ones that will help us to get things done. In particular, we are going to look at the functions that are able to help us change, create, delete, or retrieve the data that we need along the way.

With this in mind, the four functions of the database that we want to spend our time on are going to include:

1. Create an object (CRTOBJ): This one is going to help us to define a routine that will add a record over to the file that we have. It is also going to help us to do some processing to check that the record is not already something that exists before we update that record in the database.

2. Change object (CHGOBJ): This one is going to help us to define a routine to update the record that is already in the file. It is going to include all of the necessary processing to check that the record already exists before we try to update the record of the database.

3. Delete object (DLTOBJ): This one is going to help us to define a routine that will delete a record out of a file of the database. It is going to be where we will process

this through and check whether that is a record that is still on the file before we delete it along the way.

4. Retrieve object (RTVOBJ): This one is going to help us to define a routine to retrieve one or more objects or records from the file in the database. The processing can be specified for each record that is read when we modify the action diagram that comes with the function as well.

This is just the start of what we are able to do with some of these functions. But we can already see where they are going to come into good use and be worth our time to learn a little bit more about as well. These functions are great for doing a lot of the different things that we need in our files so that they work well in some of the work that we are doing with our database.

Using Expressions

Another thing that we are able to explore when it comes to the database is the expression. An expression in SQL is going to be a string that is able to make up either all or part of a statement in SQL. For example, if we are using the FindFirst method on a Recordset object, we are going to find that this is an expression that will consist of the selection criteria that are found in the WHERE command.

These expressions can help us to get a lot of the work done when we are handling some of our data online. You will find that these can help us to evaluate some of the functions that we were talking about before and even perform some of the simple math as we would like. And all of the operations that use the SQL expressions in the Microsoft Access database engine are going to be defined with the help of the VBA expression service.

Some of the Common Commands in SQL

Now it is time for us to take a look at some of the most common commands that we are able to use when it is time to work with the SQL language. There are a lot of commands to work with, and it is often going to depend on what you would like to gather up or do with the database ahead of time. Remember that this is a type of coding language that has been designed in order to help us manage, in any manner that we would like, some of the data that has been stored in the relational databases.

This means that this kind of language is going to operate through some simple, declarative statements. This just shows us that the data is going to always be secure and accurate, and it will help the program to maintain some of the integrity of the database, no matter what size it is in the first place, or how big it will get in the future.

1. ALTER TABLE: This one is going to help us to add in some of the columns that we would like to have in the database.

2. AND: This one is going to help us to combine together two conditions to meet our needs. We have

to make sure that the conditions, both of them, are true in order to get that row to be included in the results that are sent back to us.

3. AS: This one is going to be a keyword that helps sus to rename a column or a table with the help of an alias.

4. CREATE TABLE: This one is going to help us to create the new table that we want inside of a database. This helps us to specify the table name, as we wish to call it, and the name of each of the columns that show up in the table as well.

5. DELETE: This one is going to be a statement that we would use in order to remove one or more rows out of the table that we are working with.

6. GROUP BY: This one is going to be a clause that we can use in SQL to help us out with some aggregate functions. It is often going to be used along with the SELECT statement so that we are able to arrange the data that is identical into groups to look for later on.

7. INSERT: This is a statement that is going to be used when we would like to add a new row to our table.

8. IS NULL / IS NOT NULL: These are going to be the operators that are used along with the WHERE clause to help us test out whether there are some empty values found in the database.

9. ORDER BY: This is going to be a clause that will indicate to the database that you would like to sort out the results set by a particular column. You can choose whether you would like to do this numerically or alphabetically.

10. SELECT: This one is going to be a statement that is used in order to fetch any of the information that you would like from the database. Every query that you would like to use, just like we talked about before, is going, to begin with, this command.

11. SUM: This is going to be an example of a function that you can use. This one, in particular, is going to take the name of a column as the argument and then will return the sum of all of the values that you find in that column.

12. UPDATE: This is a statement that is going to allow you to edit some of the rows that are found in the table.

13. WHERE: This is going to be another example of a clause that will indicate how you would like to filter out the result set to help us only include the rows where the condition that you set is going to be seen as true.

14. WITH: This is going to be a clause that will help us to store the result of a query, usually in a table that is temporary and comes with an alias. You are also able

to define multiple temporary tables using a comma and with one instance of the WITH keyword if you would like. We will find that this clause is often going to be known as a common table expression and can help with subquery factoring as well.

The Operators and Predicates
We can also take a look at some of the different operators and predicates that we are able to add to some of the searches that we want to do when working with the SQL language. First, we are going to look at some of the operators that we are able to use. These should be familiar if you have worked with some other coding languages in the past, but we are still going to take a moment to look at them. Some of the standard relational operators that you are able to work within your coding will include:

1. Equals
2. Greater than or equal to
3. Less than or equal to
4. Less than
5. Greater than
6. Not equal to.

Notice that when you are working with a combined relation, for example, less than or equal to or greater than or equal to, we need to make sure that we always put the equal sign as the last sign in this kind of relation. This will ensure that the compiler knows what we are doing and will bring up the results that we are looking for here.

Then it is time for us to take a look at what is known as the predicates in this kind of language. These predicates are going to be a type of expression in SQL that is able to evaluate a search condition as either TRUE or FALSE and sometimes as UNKNOWN depending on the code that we are trying to write out.

The TRUE means that we see that the expression is correct based on our conditions, and then the FALSE is going to mean that the expression is not right. Then there is the possibility for UNONWN, which means that the expression is not going to be true or false in this situation. All of the values that are used in SQL as a predicate need to be compatible data types for us to compare them to one another. Some of the predicates that we are able to use in this kind of language will include:

1. All of the comparisons that we want, including greater than less than, and the other options that we did above with the operators.
2. NULL
3. IN / NOT IN
4. EXISTS / NOT EXISTS
5. LIKE BETWEEN

Day 5: The SQL Server

Today, we are going to spend some time taking a look at some of the steps that we are able to use when it is time to handle the SQL server and get it to work for our own needs. There are a number of things that we need to do to make this chapter as effective as possible, and we are going to jump right in and look at how we can make this happen below!

How to Install the Oracle Database

The first part of this process that we are going to take a look at is how we are able to install and work with the Oracle database. There are a number of options that we are able to work with. We need to first make sure that we are on the website for Oracle so that you can get the installer. After you have the installation files, which should be in the format of a zip file, then you will need to do an extraction to get them to be on the folder that you want on your computer.

From here, we need to double-click so that you can get the setup.exe file that you have to start up the installation process. Most of the following steps that we are going to work with will go through the process automatically. But we are going to divide them up into 9 steps so that you can better see how they work and what you are able to do with them.

1. The installer is going to start by asking you to provide the email address that you want. This allows you to get the latest in updates and security issues sent right to you. Clicking on the next button though will allow you to skip this part.

2. The installer is then going to ask you whether or not you would like to create and configure a new database if you want to install the software for the database only, or go through and upgrade a database that you already have. Because you are installing the Oracle database for the first time, we are going to pick out option one and then click on Next.

3. The installer will also allow you to choose the system class. Because you are installing this on your computer, rather than on a server, you will choose to go with the desktop-class and click on the Next button.

4. This fourth step is going to allow you to specify which Windows user account you would like to install and then configure for the Oracle Home to give you more security. The best option here is to usually go with the option for "Use Windows Built-in Account."

5. In this step, you are going to choose a few things. The first one is to choose which folder you would like to install this new database. The second is to choose the global name that you want for the database. And then, finally, we need to choose the pluggable database name we want to go with.

6. Once we have those things down, the installer is going to go through and do its own prerequisite check.

7. Now the installer is going to show you a summary of the information that you have, including information on the database and the global information. Mae sure to review the information to see if it is how you would like it. You can then click on the Install button if it all looks good.

8. The installer in this step is going to start installing this database. It may take a few minutes. The speeds will vary based on how fast your computer can go with this.

9. Once the installation has had some time to complete, the installer is going to show you that this is done. You can click on the button to close up the window at this point.

Installing the SQL Developer
The next thing that we are able to work with is installing and starting up your SQL developer. This is not going to require the installer, so that will make it a bit easier to work with.

But to get started on this developer, you will need to work with some kind of unzip tool of your choice. We have to make sure that we are not installing this developer onto an existing ORACLE_HOME. You will not be able to uninstall it later on when we are doing with the Oracle Universal Installer.

If you are going with one of the pre-release versions of the SQL Developer, and if you would like to continue going with one of these versions after you are done installing the official release kit, you will need to go through and unzip the official release kit in a separate folder to the one you used for the pre-release version.

The Oracle Database may be installed on your computer, and if this is true, then you will be able to find a version of this program also included. You would then be able to access it through the menu system that is on Oracle, which can make things a bit easier to work with. This particular version of the SQL developer is going to be separate from the other one that we have been talking about so far, so you will need to consider which version you would rather work with.

For the Windows system, though, there are going to be two kits that you are able to work with. One is going to be for the systems that work with the Sun Java SDK that is version 1.5 0_06 or later .and then there is a kit that works for the later versions as well. You need to double-check which version is going to be the best for your needs.

Before you go through the steps to install this developer, we need to look at some of the versions that we want to work with and more. The steps that we need to work with when it is time to install this developer is going to be depending on whether you are using the Windows system with the Sun Java SDK 1.5 0_06 or later installed or not. For both of these, though, you will find that going through and getting the file and following the steps that are needed to unzip it will be the best way to ensure that you get things to work the way that you would like.

Creating a System Connection

At some point, you will connect to the database with the help of the SQL developer that we talked about above. The database connection is going to be one of the objects that will specify the necessary information that will help you to connect the database that you would like to someone who is able to use that database. You need to make sure that there are at least one of these connections, whether it is imported, created, or existing, in order to work with this developer.

To help us create a database connection, there are a few different steps that we will need to follow to see it happen. Some of the best steps to follow will include:

1. When we are in Connections navigator in SQL, we need to be able to right-click on the Connections node and then select the New Connection. This dialog box is going to appear on your computer screen, and you should see the tab for Oracle displaying here.

2. Then there is some information that we need to add to this part. First, in the Connection Name field, we need to enter the name that we would like to have for this connection. Then in the Username field, we need to be able to enter the name of the user for whom we are creating this connection to the database. Then the Password field and the Connection Type need to be filled in.
    a. There are a few different connection types that we are able to work with, including Basic, TNS, LDAP, Advanced, and Local/Bequeath.

b. When you have chosen the connection type that you want to work with, the fields are going to change up so that they are ready for the right connection type.

3. We need to take a look at how these are going to change. If we are using the Basic type of connection, we are going to see a few changes including:
   a. In the Role field, we will be able to select out either SYSDBA or Default based on the role that has been assigned to the user.
   b. In the field for the Hostname, we will be able to enter the name of the host where we will find this database.
   c. Then we move on to the Port field. This is where we are going to enter the port of our database.
   d. Then we are in the SID field. This is where we are going to enter the SID for the database. This is when the database connection for a non-CDB user.
   e. In the Service name field, we can enter the product name for all the components of the plug-in list. This could include some things like the domain name when the database connection ends up being for the PDB user.

4. In addition, we have the option to go through and click on the Test. This helps us to test that all of the data that we already went through and provided will be able to allow the user you would like onto the

database and can form the connection you are hoping for.

5. When you are done testing this, and it is all set up, you can click on Connect in order to connect with the help of that new database connection, or you can click on Save to help save the database creation that you would like.

Running a Statement

Now that we have all of the database set up and ready to get going, it is time for us to do some of the work that we need on this system. We are going to look at a few options, such as running a statement inserting rows and storing things on the database. But we need to start out with some of the steps of running a statement on this system.

To start with this one, we need to open up a new SQL Worksheet. Then we are able to click on the arrow that is to the right of the button to open up the worksheet so that you are able to see what connections are present there. Make sure you select the connection that you would like to use right from the beginning. This is going to open up a Worksheet under the right kind of connection. If the connection isn't in the current session that you are, then you will receive a prompt to get the password to set up this connection.

Once you have that Worksheet open, you are able to use some of the standard techniques that you are used to seeing with SQL in order to either enter or edit one of these statements. As you work on entering the statements, you will notice that this SQL Developer that we set up is automatically going to apply some colors to the various elements. For example, the keywords that you use are going to show up in blue. This is going to make all of the statements a bit easier to read and understand, and will help us to find some of the errors that show up in our coding.

Any time that you enter in a statement in SQL, you will notice that the Developer is going to automatically display a list that drops down to help us enter some of these statements. This is a feature that can help provide us with some of the help that we need when entering some of the SQL keywords, table names column names, and so on.

If you spend some time experimenting with this kind of feature that is going to help you to complete your code, you may find that the Developer is not going to display the names of the columns automatically until the name of the table used by the sentence is entered. Because of this, if you want to use the functionality of code completion, you'll want to go through the table name and then work on the column names.

For the most part, though, you will find that this Developer is automatically going to display the drop-down list after you start adding in some of the statements that you would like to work with. Sometimes though, it is true that you will need to go through and manually prompt the Developer to show this list off. To do this, you can press on the Ctrl Key and the spacebar, and it will work well for you.

In addition, it is possible to work with this Developer to help automatically take some of your statements and comment or uncomment them. To make this happen, you'd have to move the line insertion point. Then, at the same time, we push the Ctrl key and the front slash. But if you would like to execute just one of the SQL statements, you would want to press on the F9 button or click the Execute Statement button that is in the toolbar for this process.

If you do the steps above and you get a statement that provides you with some data in return, then the data is going to show up in the Results tab. This will help us to get some of the information that we want out of the process and can make life a bit easier when handling some of the things that we want with our coding overall.

There are many times when you will need to work with some of these statements with your database, and the SQL Developer is going to make this process as easy to work with as possible. These statements can help to add things into the database, take them out, and so much more. Learning how to use them, and working with some of the steps that we have in this guidebook, can make it easier than ever to really make sure that you get the statements in this language to work the way that you would like.

Inserting Rows

There are also going to be some situations when we are looking at one of our tables in the database, and we will want to work with inserting some rows into the table as well. To make this happen, we are able to work with the statements of INSERT and SELECT. There are two methods that we are able to use to make this work, including:

1. We would want to work with the statement for INSERT because it can help us to list out the values we want right from one of our subqueries.
2. We would then want to work with the statement for SELECT because it can help us work with the clause of INTO here to tell the compiler where we want the information to go.

We are able to start this one out with the help of the INSERT statement. This one is going to add in one or more new rows to our table. We would be able to just use the INSERT command along with information on where we would like all of this to be added to. The INSERT statement or command is going to help us insert the data values that can be at least one, and sometimes it is possible to use them as more of these rows that are in our specific table. Then we have the column list as the name of all the columns, with a comma going in between all of them, that can then be used to help us to list out the columns so that we know where the data supply is coming from. If this is something that we take the time to add in, then the columns that show up in the table that we are in will receive the data.

The INSERT statement is not going to be able to specify all of the values that are out there. In particular, they will not be able to help us out with the following options for the columns because the SQL Server Database Engine can create its own values on these columns:

1. The columns that have an IDENTITY property are going to generate the values automatically for the column.
2. Columns that are going to use the function of NEWID as their default will be able to bring up a value for GUID that is pretty unique here.
3. Then we are able to work with some columns that we are able to get through computation. These are going to be some of the columns that are more virtual and can be defined more as one of the expressions. We are able to get these expressions with a few calculations from at least one of the other columns in the table, although this is usually going to need more work than that to make it happen. A good code that can show us how to make this happen will include:

```
CREATE TABLE TestTable
(ColA INT PRIMARY KEY,
 ColB INT NOT NULL,
 ColC AS (ColA + ColB) * 2);
```

We can take another look at how we are able to work with this as well. We are going to take a look at how we are able to place any lines in the already columned table that will be able to generate automatically the value that you need, or it will have a default value. The INSERT statement is going to help us to insert the rows that we need, the ones that have the values for some of the columns but will not do this for all of them. This is something new compared with some of the other people because, in the last one, no columns will be listed, and you will have to find the values that are the default and insert them. The coding that we are able to use for this one will include the following:

```
USE AdventureWorks2008R2;
  GO
  IF OBJECT_ID ('dbo.T1', 'U') IS NOT NULL
    DROP TABLE dbo.T1;
  GO
  CREATE TABLE dbo.T1
  (
    column_1 AS 'Computed column ' + column_2,
    column_2 varchar(30)
      CONSTRAINT default_name DEFAULT ('my column default'),
    column_3 rowversion,
    column_4 varchar(40) NULL
  );
  GO
  INSERT INTO dbo.T1 (column_4)
    VALUES ('Explicit value');
  INSERT INTO dbo.T1 (column_2, column_4)
    VALUES ('Explicit value', 'Explicit value');
  INSERT INTO dbo.T1 (column_2)
    VALUES ('Explicit value');
  INSERT INTO T1 DEFAULT VALUES;
  GO
  SELECT column_1, column_2, column_3, column_4
  FROM dbo.T1;
  GO
```

How to Store Things in the Database

While we are here, we need to take some time to look at how we will be able to take our database and use it to store some of the information that we need. This can take some time to accomplish, and it will be important for us to make sure that the data we take time working on will be able to handle being in the database without being lost at all.

We have already taken a look at how we are able to create the database that we are working with; it is time for us to look at how we are able to create one of our own scripts on the server-side that will store the form data to your MySQL. We are going to take a look at how to do this on the cloud with the help of PHP, but you will find that we are able to work with to help us get it onto that MySQL. The code that we are able to use to make all of this happen will include:

```php
<?php
// Connecting to the MySQL server
$host="mysql.yourdomain.com";
$user_name="username";
$pwd="kj67GbF54";
$database_name="visitors"; //assuming you created this
$db=mysql_connect($host, $user_name, $pwd);
if (mysql_error() > "") print mysql_error() . "<br>";
mysql_select_db($database_name, $db);
if (mysql_error() > "") print mysql_error() . "<br>";
// Storing form values into PHP variables
$fname = $_POST["fname"]; // Since method="post" in the
form
```

```php
$lname = $_POST["lname"];
$gender = $_POST["gender"];
$age = $_POST["age"];
$city = $_POST["city"];
$submitdate = date("Ymd");
// Inserting these values into the MySQL table
// we created above
$query = "insert into form_data (first_name, last_name,
gender, age, city, submit_date) values ('" . $fname . "', '" .
$lname . "', '" . $gender . "', " . $age . ", '" . $city . "', '" .
$submitdate . "')";
$result = mysql_query($query);
// mysql_query() is a PHP function for executing
// MySQL queries
echo "<h1>Thank you for submitting your details!</h1>";
?>
```

When we are trying to store some of our values in one of these kinds of tables, we need to make sure that we are doing a few things. We need to include the alphanumeric values, the data, and then the text values in the quotes. This is going to be done with three single quotes, and how we are going to see that in the code above. They are actually going to be a single quote that is followed by a double quote. The single quote is going to be important because it is going to be the final string in SQL that you can work with.

We are able to use this kind of code and more in order to see the results that you want. You will find that this helps us to take all of the data that we have and will make it easier to store inside of all the databases that you are working with, helping you to set it up for later.

How to Run SQL from a File

Another thing that we are going to take a look at is how to run Transact-SQL from the script files that we are working with. We are going to learn how to create this kind of file, how to run it, and how to save the output to the right text file that we want to work with.

First, we need to work with the command of sqlcmd to help us run this kind of file where we need it. This is going to be a text file that is able to hold onto a combination of the Transact-SQL statements, the commands that you need for the sqlcmd, and then some of the variables that are needed in the scripting variables as well.

So, to get this started, we need to go through and create our own script file to make this happen. We are able to do this with the help of the Notepad. The steps that we are able to use for it will include:

1. Click on the Start button on your computer. Point over to All Programs. In there, we are going to click on the Accessories and then click on the Notepad as well.
2. When the Notepad is open in Windows, we are going to want to copy and then past the code below:

```
USE AdventureWorks2012;
GO
SELECT p.FirstName + ' ' + p.LastName AS 'Employee Name',
a.AddressLine1, a.AddressLine2 , a.City, a.PostalCode
FROM Person.Person AS p
   INNER JOIN HumanResources.Employee AS e
      ON p.BusinessEntityID = e.BusinessEntityID
   INNER JOIN Person.BusinessEntityAddress bea
      ON bea.BusinessEntityID = e.BusinessEntityID
   INNER JOIN Person.Address AS a
      ON a.AddressID = bea.AddressID;
GO
```

When this code is added to Notepad, we will want to save it into our C drive as the myScript.sql so that we are able to find it later. At this time, we will be able to run the script file. To do this, open up the window for the command prompt. Then we can type out, in that command prompt, "sqlcmd -S myServer\instanceName -I C:\myScript.sql " Press Enter to continue.

When you are done with this one, you are going to end up with a list of the employee names of Adventure Works, along with their addresses. This should come up in the command prompt window if you went through and did the rest of the coding properly.

To finish this one off, we want to make sure that we are able to save the output that we have over to a text file. This will ensure that we are able to get through with this and see the option that we would like to work with later and bring it out without having to do all of the codings again. The steps that we need to do in order to save the output over to a text file, and this will include:

1. Open up the command prompt window that you have.
2. When you are in that window, and it is all set up, we will want to type in sqlcmd -S myServer\instanceName – C"\yscript.sql -o C:\EmpAdds.txt.
3. Press Enter when you are done.

With this one, you will find that the command prompt is not going to return any kind of output to you. Instead, the output is going to be sent over to the file that we listed above. You can double-check that this is what happened by going into the file for EmpAdds.txt and seeing if the output that we did above was actually saved for you or not.

Deleting the System Connection

And finally, we are going to take a look at how to delete the system and the views that we are able to work with. We are able to delete or drop some of the views that come with our SQL Server. Before you do this, though, we have a few limitations and restrictions that we are able to remember here. When you drop a view, the definition that you get with the view, along with the other information about the view will be deleted out of the catalog for the system. All of the permissions that you see with the view are going to be deleted as well. In addition, any of the view that is on the table that will be dropped with the DROP TABLE command need to be dropped with the explicit use of the DROP VIEW.

Now we are able to take a look at how we are able to delete these things out of the database as we go along. To delete a view from the database, we will need to take a look at some of the steps below:

1. We first need to get into the part known as Object Explorer. From here, we are able to expand out the database that contains the view that you are hoping to delete. From that part then, we need to expand out the folder for Views.
2. At this point, we can right-click on the view that we would like to delete before clicking on the button there for Delete.
3. In the dialog box that shows up for Delete Object, we can just click on OK in order to make it happen.

Another option that we are able to work with is the Transact-SQL. To make this one, we need to take a look at a few of the options that we are able to work with includes:

1. In the Object Explorer and then we are able to connect it to the instance that shows up for the Database Engine.

2. Then we can move to the Standard bar and click on a New Query.

3. Then we are able to copy and paste the code that we are able to work with the following code in order to help us to get things done. And then we will click on the Execute it. The example that we are going to do here is going to delete the specified view only if the view is already in existence. The code that we need here is going to include:

USE AdventureWorks2012 ;

GO
IF OBJECT_ID ('HumanResources.EmployeeHireDate',
'V') IS NOT NULL
DROP VIEW HumanResources.EmployeeHireDate;
GO

When we go through and delete some of the parts that we need out of the database, we need to be careful. We are not able to go back through and add them back in if we would like. So we need to use caution and make sure that we are only deleting the things that we need during this time.

Day 6: Users and Roles

One of the things that we will need to focus on when we are handling some of our databases and what we are able to do with all of this is to look at who is allowed to gain access to the database, what each person on the database is allowed to do, and so on. If you have a large database that your customers are able to get onto, it is likely that you want to go through and set up some limitations, for example, so that they are not able to make major changes to what is on the database overall. This chapter is going to take some time to look at the users and the roles of your database, and how you are able to get these set up for some of your own needs as well.

Logins to the Server

The first thing that we will take a look at is how we are able to log into one of our servers with SQL. You are able to do this with the help of the command prompt on your computer, or by use of any of the graphical management tools that you have. When you do go through and log into an SQL server instance using the administration tools, though, you are going to be prompted to answer a few things like adding in the server name, the login for the SQL Server, and a password.

You can also go through and log into this with the help of Windows Authentication. With this option, you will not need to provide this information each time that you get onto the server because you are able to use the information from your Windows account to do this automatically. If your server is running in the authentication for mixed-mode, and you log in with the SQL Server Authentication, then you have to work with the password and log in as we talked about before. It is usually suggested that you work with Windows Authentication if possible.

Sometimes when you go through this process, you will need to spend some time verifying the connection protocol that you have. When you do connect over to the Database Engine, you will need to go through and work with some query in order to help check out the current connection and to ensure that you are going to get the authentication method. If you use this query well, you will be able to tell if the connection you are using is encrypted or not.

SELECT net_transport, auth_scheme, encrypt_option
FROM sys.dm_exec_connections
WHERE session_id = @@SPID;

And that is all that you need to do to make sure that you are able to log into your own SQL database. If you spend time looking over the Windows Authentication, the process is even easier because you can be logged in automatically if you are already using your Windows account, but the other options are going to be important to all of this as well and will work out if you choose to go with them as well.

Assigning Roles in the Database

We need to make sure that we take some time to assign roles in the database. There are some people who should just get the most basic access to the database, and then some who are going to be in control of running the database and making changes. And there are often a lot of different things that show up in between when it comes to the roles and the access points of the people who can be on that database.

You are able to spend some time grouping privileges in the database roles with the help of Oracle. Instead of an object owner going through and individually granting privileges to one or more of the users, especially when they have a similar description of the job that they do, the object owner is able to create a role and then grant that over when needed.

For example, maybe you are an administrator for a database for a big retailer. Each day, some new store clerks are going to be hired. The application of your database at the time is going to allow them the option of doing a dozen different requirements, and these can include:

1. INSERT into the table for sales.
2. UPDATE the table for inventory when it is needed.
3. DELETE from the table of orders as well.

There are going to be a few roles that are already created and set up when it is in the database, which is going to make it easier to manage some of the tasks that are out there. You can choose to add in some more if you would like along the way, but these are the basics that will make it easier if you are just looking for something to get started with along the way. Some of the roles that Oracle is going to supply to you when the database is first installed will include:

1. Connect: This is going to include all of the privileges that are needed to ensure that someone is able to connect with that database.
2. Resource: This one is going to include a lot of the roles that a developer is able to use to help create and manage an application, such as altering and creating many types of objects, including tables, sequences, and views.

3. Recovery_catalog_owner: This is going to allow the grantee to come through and administer the Oracle Recovery Manager catalog.

4. Scheduler_Admin: This one is going to allow the grantee the option to manage the Oracle job scheduler.

5. DBA: This one is going to help provide a user with many of the major privileges that are required to help administer the database. These can manage the users, the security, the space, the parameters of the system, and even some of the backups that should happen as well.

As the administrator of your own database, you need to consider what kinds of access you would like to assign to the different people who are going to get onto your system. The decisions that you make will often depend on the information that is going to be found on the database, and even some of the different people who you think will be there as well. This will make it easier to have more control over the database and who is able to access it, make changes, and more.

Commands to Help with Users and Roles

With some of this in mind, we are going to spend a moment to look at a few more of the commands that we have not had the time to look over yet in this guidebook. These commands are going to help you with some of the different user roles and more that you have, and some of the other administrative tasks that you would want to focus your attention on here as well. Some of the other options that we need to spend our time here will include:

1. LIKE: This is going to be the special operator that we are able to use along with the WHERE clause. It is a good one to help us find the specific patterns that are going to show up in our column.

2. AVG: This is the command that we are going to use when we want to make sure that we are able to get the average function for any of our columns that are numeric at the time.

3. ROUND: This is going to be a type of function that is able to take the name of the column as an integer as the arguments. It is going to round the values in the column to the number of decimal places that is specified by the integer.

4. SUM: Then, we can move on to the SUM function. This one is going to be able to take its argument from the name of the column and then will allow us to return the sum of all of the values that we are able to find in that column.

5. MAX: This one is going to be the function that is able to take the name of a column and use that as its argument. It is then able to return the largest value to this column, as well.

6. MIN: This is the final function that we are going to take a look at, and it is going to help us take the name of a column as the main argument that we want to work with and then will return the smallest value that is in that column at the time.

Day 7: Tables and Data Modification

One of the things that you will spend a lot of time working on when it comes to your database and the SQL language is working with a lot of tables, and making some modifications to the information that is found in those tables as well. This is why we are going to devote our last day of this course to looking more into these tables and how we are able to use them, add data to them, and make some modifications to ensure that it will work the way that we want throughout the database.

What is a Table in SQL?

The first place to start here is a look at what the SQL tables are going to be all about. The data that we need in our database is going to be stored inside of one of these tables and then added to our database. A single database can be large, and could potentially hold onto hundreds of these tables. Each table is going to have its own unique role when it comes to the schema of the database.

While the schema and the architecture of the database are going to be concepts that are higher up than what we are going to explore in this chapter, you will find that they are going to help us to create the right tables for our needs, and get some good results in the process.

When you create your own table in this language, you will find that they are going to be comprised of rows and columns. The columns in the table are going to be responsible for storing a variety of data types, like files, dates, texts, and numbers. There are even a lot of different types of columns that we are able to add to the table, and the types of data that we are going to use will often vary depending on how the developer created the SQL table.

Then we are able to work with a table row as well. This one is going to be a horizontal record of values that are all going to fit into each of the columns of the table. When both of these are able to come together, you will find that it can provide you with the information that you need to ensure that you will see the best results as well.

Before we move on, though, we need to take a look at how we are able to create one of these tables through the use of a query. The coding that we will need for this one is below:

```
USE mydatabase;

CREATE TABLE orders
(id INT IDENTITY(1,1) PRIMARY KEY,
customer VARCHAR(50),
day_of_order DATETIME,
product VARCHAR(50),
quantity INT);
```

The first line that we see here is going to show us where we are going to get the scope of our query ad will direct the SQL to run the command against that object that we can create. Then the blank line that we are able to see here is going to be something that is not required, but we add it in to help with some of the readability that is there.

Then we can move on to the line that starts with CREATE. This is a clause that has to be there because it is going to tell SQL that we would like it to create a new table at this point. And with the code above, we are going to name that table orders. You are able to name it anything that you would like.

Each of the columns in the table is going to come with their own guidelines, and the code above that we put inside of the parenthesis is going to tell SQL how to go about setting up these guidelines. The columns of the table are often going to be shown in a list format, and then we are able to separate these with a comma as well. For now, the most important thing that we need to focus on is making sure that we know that with the code above, we are creating a new, empty table in SQL that is going to go by the name of orders, and it has five columns total.

And that is as simple as it can be! We are able to go in and add in a lot of other features to the mix if we would like. But we can also keep it this simple to ensure that we get some of the results that we would like as well. You can make the table bigger or smaller, add in more parts or take them away. And in the next few sections, we will take a look at some more things that we can do with the table as well. But being able to create a simple table is going to be a great way to get started as well.

How to Insert a Data

Next, we need to take a look is to insert some data into that table that we just went through and created. We are going to work with the INSERT command to help us to draw up a query that is going to insert some of the data that we need into that orders table that we did before. The coding that we need to make this happen is going to be below:

USE mydatabase;

INSERT INTO orders
(customer, day_of_order, product quantity)
VALUES('Tizag', '8/1/08', Pen', 4

If we go through and use this in the proper manner, you will find that all of the information that we have above about that customer will show up in the first row of the table that we created above. We can go through this and add in all of the information that we need for all five columns, or more if we are working with another table, in order to make sure that this is going to fill up the database in the manner that we would like.

Doing a Bulk Insert

The next thing that we need to take a look at is how we are able to do a bulk insert of our information. We have spent some time so far looking at how we are able to add in information to just a few of the columns of our table. But if we need to add in a lot of information to the table, that process can be really hard and take too long. That is why we need to work with the process of creating our own bulk insert as well.

This is a simple process to work with, but you will be able to go through and add in as many columns and such as you would like to this kind of table to make it work the way that you would like.

While we are here, we can take a look at some of the arguments that will show up in this kind of coding. The first one is going to be the database name, which is going to be the name that we will have for the specified table or view and where the view is going to reside. If you do not specify this, it is going to be the current database.

Then we can work with the schema name, which is going to be the name of the table or the view schema. This one is going to be optional if the schema for the user performing the bulk-import operation is the schema of the specified table or view. If the schema is not specified and the default schema of the user performing the bulk operation is different from the view or the table that you are specifying, then the server is going to return an error message, and this will all be canceled for you.

Then there is the table name. This one is going to be the name of the table or view to import all of the data into. Only views in which all the columns use the same base table can be used on this one. We can then move on to the data file. This is going to be the full path of the file of data that is going to contain data to import into the view or the table that you would like. A BULK INSERT is able to import the data from either Azure Blob storage or a disk, which can include a floppy disk, network, and even a hard dis.

The data file that you are working with needs to have a valid path specified on the server which this is going to run. If this ends up being a remote file that you are using, then you will need to spend some time specifying the Universal Naming Convention to get it to work.

Deleting Data

There will be some times when you are doing the work in your database, and you decide that you need to delete a specific part, or sometimes even the whole database that is there. In order to make this happen, you would need to work with the SQL DELETE statement. This is going to be the option that we can use in order to delete the existing records that are on a table that you have. The syntax that we are able to work with to make this happen will include;

DELETE FROM table name WHERE condition;

We can add more to this if we would like, but this is a basic option to get us started and will ensure that we are going to be able to get the results that we would like overall. One thing to remember with this one, though, is that we need to use caution when deleting the records on the table. We have to notice the WHERE clause in this statement. This is going to be the part that will specify which records we would like to have deleted in the table. If you do not add in this clause, then you will delete the whole table. If that is what you would like to do in the first place, then that is fine, but if you just want to delete a few records, make sure that WHERE clause is put inside.

What is the process of Truncate?

Another option that we are able to work with is the TRUNCATE command. This one is a bit different than some of the others but can still provide us with some neat work that we are able to do in our database. To start with, this process is going to help us remove all of the rows from a table, or even from special parts of the table, without having to log the individual row deletions as we go through.

TRUNCATE TABLE, like we are going to discuss in this section, is going to be similar to the statement of DELETE, without the WHERE clause like we did above, but it is faster and will not use up as many systems and transaction log resources. If you know that you need to delete the whole table or a lot of the information that is inside of it, then this is most likely the right one for you to choose to use here.

We can take a look at the syntax that is necessary to get this one started below:

-- Syntax for SQL Server and Azure SQL Database

TRUNCATE TABLE
  { database_name.schema_name.table_name |
schema_name.table_name | table_name }
   [WITH (PARTITIONS ({
<partition_number_expression> | <range> }
   [, ...n]))]
[;]

<range> ::=
<partition_number_expression> TO
<partition_number_expression>

There are going to be a few arguments that you are able to work with on this one. First, the database_name is going to be the name that you choose to give the database. Then we have the schema_name, which is going to be the name of the schema that you have the table in to start with. Then there is table_name, that is going to be the name of the table that you would like to truncate, or to remove all the rows from. We have to make sure that the table name is literal here for it to work. You cannot use an OBJECT_ID() function or any kind of variable to do this.

We are going to work with the part that is known as the <partition_number_expression) as well. There are multiple ways that we are able to specify this one, and some of them will include the following:

1. We are able to go through and provide it with the number of partitions that we would like to work with. We can write it out something like the following WITH (PARTITIONS (2))
2. We can go through and provide it with the partition numbers for several of the individual partitions that we want to handle, and then separate it out with some commas. So this one would like something like this WITH (PARTITIONS (1, 5))
3. We can even go through and provide both the ranges and the individual's partitions. A good example of how this one would work would be something like the following WITH (PARTITIONS (2, 4, 6 TO 8))

There are a few times when we will want to work with the TRUNCATE TABLE option rather than the DELETE statement that we talked about above. First, we will find that the latter is going to use up less log space, which can be ideal for a lot of businesses. The DELETE statement is going to take its tie, removing one row at a time and then will record this entry into the transaction log when it is done. The TRUNCATE TABLE is going to remove the data when it deallocates the pages of the data used in order to store the table records and data, and only the page of that is going to show up in the transaction log, saving a lot of tie and hassle.

There are also going to be fewer locks that are going to be used. When we execute out the DELETE statement, we will use a row lock. This means that each row contained in the table will need to be locked so that we are able to delete it properly. When working with the TRUNCATE TABLE, it is always going to lock the table and the page, but it will not go through and lock up each individual row in the process.

Without any exceptions, there will not be any pages that are left in the table. After we have been able to work with the statement for DELETE, our table is going to end up with a few pages that are empty. In this case, the empty pages that we do end up with are going to be shown in a heap, and we have to add in at least an exclusive table lock to help deallocate them, or it will not work. You will find that the operation for the delete function is not going to work here, and the table is going to hold onto a lot of empty pages along the way. For the indexes, the delete operation can leave some of these empty pages behind, even though these are going to be deallocated quickly with some of the cleanup processes that are happening in the background.

When you work with the TRUNCATE TABLE, though you will find that it is able to remove all of the rows from the table, the structure of our table and its columns, constraints, indexes, and so on are going to remain in place. To make sure that we are able to remove the data definition along with some of its data, we are able to work with the DROP TABLE statement as well.

How to Merge Your Data

It is also possible for us to go through and merge some of the data that we have in our tables. This can help if we are working with cases of duplicate data in the table, or if we would like to be able to combine two tables into one to either update it or to make a brand new one.

Before you do some of the mergings, though, we need to make sure that we are really paying attention to some of the work that we are doing here. If we do not merge the tables properly, then we may end up ruining the data and losing some of the information that we really need in these situations, as well. We want to make sure that we are combining the right parts of the table together to make the new one and that we are not losing information in the process.

How to Combine and Join Tables

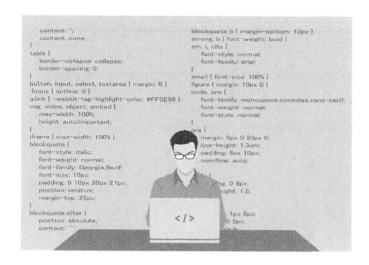

There are some situations when you are working with your data when you will want to merge it into one or merge at least a few columns into one. We are going to look at how we are able to run inserts, updates, and remove operations from the effects of the join with the origin table on the target column. For example, we can use this to help us to synchronize two tables when we delete, update, or insert rows into one table based on some of the differences that may show up in the other table along the way.

The conditional behavior that shows up when we use the MERGE statement is going to work best when we have two tables that are going to come up with a mixture of characteristics that do match with each other. To help us with this, if we try to insert in a new row when it doesn't exist in in the first place, or we would like to update a row when it isn't going to match up in our code, it is going to show up the way we want. But when we just want to update one of the tables in the database and have it use the information that is found in the rows of an additional table, you would be able to prove the performance and the scalability of this with some of the basic commands in this process including INSERT, DELETE< and UPDATE statements.

The code that we are able to use for this is pretty long, but it is going to help us to handle a lot of what we need to do when it comes to the coding we would like to accomplish. It is going to help us to set up the temporary name that we need with all of this, using the WITH <common_table_expression> part. This is going to also make sure that we are staying within the scope of our specific MERGE statement that we spent our time with.

Another thing that we need to take a look at with this one is the TOP expression. This one is going to specify the percentage or number of rows that are going to be affected by this. It can either show up as a percentage or a number depending on the tables that you are trying to combine. This clause is something that is going to apply after the whole source table, and the target table that you are using is able to join, and then we know that the rows are not going to have any kind of insert, update, or delete action on them.

This kind of clause is also going to reduce how many joined rows go to a certain value. The insert, delete and update actions or commands are going to be distributed among the actions that we are able to define when we bring in the

WHEN clauses. For example, if we specify something like TOP (10), it is going to affect ten rows. Of these, 7 may be the ones that we update, 3 are inserted, and 1 deleted and soon.

Because the statement for MERGE is going to work on a full table scan the two tables we're going to work with, sometimes we will see the I/O performance affected when we use this clause to change a large table by creating multiple batches. When this happens, make sure that all of the successive batches that we use target the new rows.

Doing an Outer Join

While we are in this chapter, we need to spend some time taking a look at what an outer joint is all about. This is going to be a specific construction of a query that is going to be set up to make for more arrays than usual. The process of building up the specific queries that we need in SQL to get to a database is going to be really technical, and the outer join is going to help us to work with some of the details that we need for all of this to come together.

A programmer who is trying to write out a query is able to work with either a right or a left outer join in order to include table results that only come with a given kind of component, rather than having to see more components present. A left outer join is going to help us include all of the rows that we need in the table, regardless of whether that position column has some results in it or not. Then the inner join is going to require that both of the components have to be present to work.

Because these joins are going to provide for some ore diversity, they are going to be found in a lot of the searches that are less rigid and will not require some strict adherence to the concept of having consistent data from multiple components of the search that we are doing.

Conclusion

Thank you for making it through to the end of *SQL Programming*. Let's hope it was able to provide you with all the tools you need to achieve your goals.

The next step is to get to work with creating some of your own databases and being able to use the SQL language to help you get all of the work done in no time. This is a great language to work with, and as we were able to go through a few of the codes that you are able to use in this database, you can quickly see why it is such a great one to work with. SQL gets right to the point and ensures that we are able to work with our database in any manner that we would like.

There are many businesses that will want to create, modify, and work with one of these databases for some of their own needs. It allows them to keep track of their customers, to make sure that their orders are placed in the right, to show off some of the products that they want to sell, and more. There are a lot of reasons to work with a database, but it will not take long to figure out that they can grow large, and you need some method to help keep the management of that database in line along the way.

This guidebook is meant to help you to get all of that done and more. We took a look at many of the commands, codes, and other parts that you need to really make sure that your database is going to behave the way that you want. Even if you haven't been able to do much work with the databases in the past, you will find that with the tips and tricks and codes that we handle in this guidebook, you will be able to really get some of the work done that you would like on that database, and your management skills of that information will go through the roof.

We split this information up into seven days so that you can learn the information and get it down in no time. Don't let the fear of a large database scare you. Tackle it right on with the help of the SQL language, and all that this is able to offer to you along the way. Taking this process day by day will make it easier to understand what is going on with all of the parts of the database and can set you up for some of the success that you are looking for.

Many companies are going to rely on a database to help them see some of the results that they would like in no time. It helps them to keep their business organized and can ensure that all of the information that they need is going to be able to stay in order and be secure. When you're ready to learn how to work with SQL on your database to make database management easier than ever before, check out this guide to get you started.

Printed in Great Britain
by Amazon